THE C...

*A Critical and Honest Examination of
God and Religion*

Written By

BO BENNETT

www.GodTheConcept.com

eBookIt.com
365 Boston Post Road, #311
Sudbury, MA 01776

First printing–January 2011
Second printing–May 2012

publisher@ebookit.com
http://www.ebookit.com

Copyright 2012, eBookIt.com
ISBN: 978-1-4566-0004-4

~~~~~

This book is dedicated to God. Without the concept of him, this book would be pointless.

~~~~~

~~~~~

"Two roads diverged in a wood, and I—
I took the one less traveled by,
And that has made all the difference."
— Robert Frost

~~~~~

Table of Contents

Preface

Growing up, church was about as enjoyable as being thrown naked into a tub of red ants. The only time I enjoyed church was when we heard someone pass gas during the silent prayers. Or when I was hungry and got to eat that wafer thing. From high school on, I went to church only when necessary (weddings, funerals, exorcisms, etc.) and thought that anyone who believed what was being preached at church must have a few screws loose somewhere. It wasn't until about 25 years later that I would start to reevaluate my position.

My spiritual/intellectual journey began as a result of a lifetime of unanswered questions combined with a moment of reflection — I realized that many of my good friends, family members, and associates were Christian. These are intelligent and rational individuals, so how in the world, I asked myself, can they seriously believe in all the ancient myths, superstition, and supernatural events associated with the religion? Can Christianity be true? After all, I really never devoted much time to it and I never really read the Bible. Even if it were not true, who am I to take away a worldview that is apparently working for so many people? And the most important question, are better off without Christianity? These are questions I had to seriously consider before "going public" with my views.

I devoted countless hours to studying religion — Christianity in particular, which included reading the entire Bible cover to cover (New International Version). I have listened to over 1000 hours of religious debate, read many books written by both atheists and Christians, and completed dozens of courses from world's leading universities on Christianity, Catholicism, Theology, Biblical Studies, Argumentation, Historical Jesus, Cosmology, Neuroscience, Human behavior, Biology, Classic, Quantum, and Particle Physics, Philosophy of Religion, and even Apologetics.

While I am far from an expert in all these fields of study, my area of expertise is in the arguments for and against the existence of God as well as the arguments for and against the truth of Christianity. It wasn't long before I became passionate about religion and had a whole new appreciation and respect for

Christianity as well as for those who embrace Christianity — *but only for the right reasons*.

Studying the faith as an outsider has given me what I believe to be a unique perspective in which I am certain both the atheist and theist will find enlightening.

This isn't the first time I have become obsessed with a topic. In 8th grade I became obsessed with martial arts and achieved my black belt in *Kempo Karate* four years later, then my second-degree black belt in *Tae-Kwon-Do* several years after that. In 2001 I became obsessed with public speaking, joined *Toastmasters*, and completed all 40 speeches for their prestigious Distinguished Toastmasters Award in a record six months. Electric cars, computer programming, podcasting — all topics in which I became obsessed, as well as a recognized leading expert. I should also mention that my adolescent obsession with making money resulted in me selling my company for $20 million at age 29. Financial freedom is what has allowed me the opportunity to obsess full-time on the topic of religion and Christianity this last year.

Obsession, when properly directed, can be a great asset.

So what's my view on God and Christianity? Well that is what this whole book is about. In short, I do not accept the supernatural beliefs commonly associated with Christianity as being true. I studied and read the Bible with an open mind and an open heart. I prayed as suggested by my Christian friends to allow the "Holy Spirit to enlighten me" (just to make sure I was following all the rules). I carefully evaluated arguments for and against Christianity and the evidence (and lack of evidence) has led me to the conclusion that God certainly does exist, but not as being, but as a concept. While this idea may appear to invalidate all of religion, I will argue that religion, specifically Christianity, still has quite a bit to offer the human race.

This is a subject about which I am extremely passionate, so while I might appear tough on some of the Christian beliefs, it needs to be made clear that it's the *belief* I have a problem with and not the practicing Christian.

This journey of mine began not by seeking God or Jesus, but by seeking *truth*. This does not mean I was searching for the "lack of Jesus" either. I was simply searching for a better understanding of the universe, my fellow humans, and the meaning of life. If truth led to God, so be it. If truth led to a world without God, so be it.

I am fortunate enough to live a wonderful life with a loving family. I don't have any spiritual voids that require filling and I do believe that if there is a God, he gave us everything we need to solve our own problems. My purpose for devoting this stage of my life to the study of God started out from personal curiosity alone and soon developed into a desire to share what I have found with others.

My intent is not to harm Christianity in any way, but encourage more critical thinking using reason and logic. If I am "against" anything, it's the ignorance of basing ones life on a set of beliefs that he or she cannot even begin to justify. It's the accepting of ideas hammered into your head from childhood without critically examining those ideas with an adult mind. It's the idea of being so committed to something being true, one loses all ability to reason and think logically. And I am not just referring to those who are religious.

My goal for this book is to make you think about certain ideas harder than you ever did before. I want to make you question your own beliefs and think about how you came to hold those beliefs in the first place. I want you to challenge any of my ideas that do not make sense to you or ideas with which you disagree. Discuss these ideas with others, look up what others have to say on the Internet, evaluate the evidence and make your own decision based on your own careful evaluation. Let your beliefs become YOURS, whatever they may be. I have come to certain conclusions and I will certainly make them known. I hope to convince you through logic, reason, and appealing to your conscious, that adoption of the ideas I lay out in this book will lead to a positive "reformation" in traditional Christian thinking. What this means to you personally, and society in general, is described in detail throughout this book and summarized in the concluding chapters.

You might be saying to yourself, "Who do you think you are trying to change what God revealed?" As you will see throughout this book, Christianity is like one, big, 2,000-year-old game of telephone beginning with the actions and sayings of Jesus as interpreted by apostles, scribes, translators, popes, saints, and philosophers. I am simply going back to the very beginning (literally) and critically examining some of the more universally-accepted beliefs that we hold today.

As you follow me on this journey, it's my hope that you will see that the idea of divine revelation may just be a lot more human than divine.

PART I: WHAT AND WHY

Chapter 1: Science, Philosophy, and Religion: Do We Really Need All Three?

Since the beginning of recorded human history, we've seen that religion has played a large part in our development. Around 600 BCE, philosophy enters the scene and challenges us with important questions about the world and our place in it. Although some form of science has been around since humankind, in the 16th century the "Scientific Revolution" was born. Science builds and organizes knowledge in the form of testable explanations and predictions about the natural world, which, among other things, results in benefits to humankind that allows us to live longer, healthier, and happier lives. Given that we now have science, do we still need philosophy and religion? Even if we do keep them around, are they even compatible with science?

The answer to this question should be a no-brainer, however, as Americans we have the unique ability to give multiple definitions to the same term, therefore, screwing up what was once a perfectly simple concept. Let me start off by sharing with you my overly simplistic definition that shows the relationship between these concepts, then we can expand from there. *Philosophy is what we think, religion is what we believe, and science is what is.* If this is the case, we can see that all three are vital to our way of life and all three *can be* compatible when what we think, what we believe, and what is, is all the same. But unfortunately, unlike the piano keys living side-by-side on Stevie Wonder's piano keyboard, this harmony won't work for everyone.

Many people might have a problem with the idea of "what is" being determined only scientifically. For example, religious "Truth" (did you know that if you capitalize the first letter of any word it becomes indisputable?) is seen as the ultimate "what is" although no science is involved. Some sects of Christianity actually hold that we cannot trust science because Satan prevents us from knowing the real truth or we are incapable of knowing truth because of sin. But how can we trust religious truth when each religion has their own "Truths" that are incompatible with other religious "Truths"? Philosophy would also have a problem with my claim that only science can only determine *what is*. Philosophy holds that there are many truths we can uncover through philosophical thought that we could never prove scientifically; for example, the existence of God. But, of course, depending on the philosopher, philosophy can both "prove" and "disprove" the existence of God.

At the end of the day, science is the common denominator between all humans, of all faiths, who subscribe to any philosophy. Through mathematical and logical truth, most of us can agree on what actually is. Still, science falls short in providing answers that only philosophy and/or religion can answer. Why are we here? Why is there something versus nothing? Why do we ask so many "why" questions?

Expanding on philosophy and religion a bit more, philosophy essentially means *the love of wisdom usually derived from the contemplation of issues related to human existence*. However, in researching the definition of religion, I came across over 50 distinct definitions. The main reason for this, I would suggest, is that people like to define religion based on characteristics of their own belief systems. Despite the differences, the central theme to all these definitions is the same: *religion is how we understand our place in the universe and our relationship to others around us*.

There is an overlap with religion and philosophy, but religion tends to be associated with the worship of one or more deities, as well as ritualistic practices. But I would argue that these associations are not fundamental to religion and can, and often do, discourage people from appreciating what religion is really about.

Unlike philosophy, religion is more feeling-based than thought-based. When we have those moments of deep connections with the universe or other people, we are having *religious experiences*; not "philosophical experiences" or "scientific experiences". Although these types of feelings can be explained scientifically as chemical reactions in the brain, these feelings often lead to what many would consider "irrational" conclusions that are not based on logic or reason. For example, the unconditional lifelong love a father feels for his daughter when holding her for the first time, the overwhelming sense of oneness with the universe when viewing the world from the top of the Italian Alps, or gazing up at the stars and knowing that we are not alone in the universe. To claim any knowledge of "Truth" — or the existence of a supernatural being — from these kinds of experiences is to pervert the essence of religion.

What about the more widely-accepted view of religion that involves the supernatural? For many well-adjusted adults who pride themselves on critical thinking, there is no place for this kind of superstition in their worldview. But this doesn't mean that humanity would be better off without it nor does it mean that you would be a better human being by not embracing some form of it. The promise of immortality in paradise, a divine purpose, and being looked after by a heavenly father, gives hope to those who cannot find hope elsewhere, and those who may not be as emotionally strong to accept less desirable possibilities. This hope allows people to live better lives, even if the hope is grounded in fantasy.

While it's easy for the nontheist to dismiss this as "false hope" the fact is that the promises are possible — no matter how improbable — and that's what hope is all about.

So we need science, philosophy, and religion — the human experience would be lacking without any one of them. However, making all three compatible with each other is not easy, but possible. As Albert Einstein said, *"Science without religion is lame. Religion without science is blind."*

I think what he really meant to say was, *"Science without religion is lame. Religion without science is blind. Science without philosophy is unsatisfactory. Philosophy without science is visionless. Philosophy without religion is subpar. Religion without philosophy sucks big time."*

But that just didn't sound as catchy.

Chapter 2: Theists, Atheists, and Agnostics, Oh My!

So what are you? A theist, an atheist, an agnostic, or something else entirely? These definitions are subjective, commonly misunderstood, and often misused. Although it's more important to fully understand your beliefs rather than the term that is used to label you, it's generally considered a good idea to "pick a team", have good reasons to be on that team, and defend that team when necessary.

A "theist" is someone who believes in a god or many gods. These days, in most cultures, theists believe in the God of Abraham, — Christians, Jews, and Muslims. "The" God is believed to have many attributes such as omniscience, omnipotence, omnibenevolence, and other "omnis". Within the theist category, there are many sub categories based on your degree of certainty, attributes you assign to God, etc. But in general, as a theist, you are either a believer of this commonly accepted definition of the Abrahamic God, or a believer in many gods.

An "atheist" is the opposite of a theist (thus the "a" before "theist"). This simply means you don't believe in a God or gods. Unfortunately for atheists, this term has become synonymous with militant pagans determined to destroy all that is good in the world.

Many see the atheist as one who is *certain* there is no God. The idea that anyone can have complete knowledge of the universe (and beyond) to assert that there is no God is foolish. However, philosophically one can argue that the theistic God *certainly* cannot *logically* exist based on supposed conflicting attributes. This argument is only true if this God is bound to the laws of logic. If you do adopt the label "atheist" be prepared to clarify your position and accept the many negative connotations and dirty looks that go along for the ride. While there are many different degrees of atheism, most atheists are pretty darn confident the Abrahamic God does not exist. The term "nontheism" is synonymous with atheism, but avoids the many negative connotations that accompany it.

An "agnostic" is someone who claims they do not know — or cannot know — if God exists or not. I would suggest that everyone is agnostic, even those who think they know for certain that God exists. Even if someone were to claim God spoke to him or her directly and asserted it was God, it's possible that it could have been Satan, an advanced alien being capable of mind manipulation and control, or that person's dead great Aunt Edna playing a practical joke. Certainty about the non-existence or existence of God is something we simply cannot have.

Some claim that agnosticism is a "cop out" since it does not really choose a side. I can see that. Despite the fact that we may all be agnostic in one sense, agnosticism is usually seen as a more politically correct form of atheism where non-belief in God is implied unless otherwise stated. Like atheists, agnostics have varying degrees of belief, but are generally closer to belief than the atheist.

So what are you? Keep in mind that the label is not really as important as thought and fair evaluation that go into adopting the belief system, which the label represents. Equally important is your ability to speak eloquently, diplomatically, and convincingly about your belief system. This effort will encourage religious understanding and tolerance, which is something this world certainly needs.

PART II: ARGUMENTS

Chapter 3: The Meaning of Life

I've heard it said that if there is no God, then life has no meaning. This is a gross misrepresentation of the word "meaning" and belittles human existence to the billions of people who don't believe in a creator. God or no God, it's YOU that gives your life meaning.

When one refers to the meaning of life, he or she refers to the purpose of us being here. Are we on this earth for a reason and if so what is that reason? It's reasonable to assume that if we were created, the creator created us for a reason. But that doesn't necessarily have to be the case. For example, I created a sandwich the other day so I could eat it. But while creating the sandwich, I also created a mess. I had no purpose for the mess. The mess was simply a byproduct of the sandwich creation.

Is it possible that we, along with all other forms of life, are simply a byproduct of the universe?

And what about animals and other life forms? Some insist that humans were created for a reason, while other life forms are nothing more than collections of amoral organic blob at our disposal. However, those who hold this view overlook the fact that at the DNA level, many life forms are very much the same as we are. If we have a purpose, it's very likely that everything else does as well. Conversely, if they don't have a purpose, we most likely don't either.

Now is a good time to make clear the difference between purpose and *divine purpose* — or, as some have called it, *intrinsic meaning*. A divine purpose is the idea that God created us for a reason. Some say this reason is to serve, worship, and glorify him. Some translate this as to "know" him or have a "relationship" with him.

In fact, the reasons are all over the board as to why God might have created us. Once again, you'll find a dozen theists with a dozen different reasons as to why. But what if there were no divine purpose and we are simply a byproduct of the universe? Does this mean we can have no purpose to our lives? Of course not.

Without divine purpose or intrinsic meaning, **we** are free to give our lives meaning. We are even free to live meaningless lives! Perhaps this *is* the work of God giving us the gift of ultimate freedom; freedom from divine purpose as well as freedom from divine consequences for our choice.

What you do with your life is your choice. Release yourself from this idea of divine dictatorship and embrace an even more perfect idea of God: one that does not require, desire, or want anything from you. You can believe in a God who has given you the power to define meaning in your own life, or believe in a life void of any God.

The end result is the same: your life, your choice, your meaning.

Chapter 4: Where Does Logic Come From?

Before one tries to use logic to evaluate the evidence for and against the existence of God and/or other religious claims, one must contemplate the nature of logic. Christian apologist (one who defends the faith) Matt Slick has asked, "How can absolute, conceptual, abstract laws be derived from a universe of matter, energy, and motion?" That's a good question.

The rational Christian answer is simple: God did it. End of story.

So, in the immortal words of Ricky Ricardo, atheists "got some splainin' to do!"

The assumption embedded in the question is that the atheist is also a *materialist*, or someone who believes that only matter (including energy) exists and even consciousness is a result of material interactions. So it's often asked, "so what then is logic made out of?" To that stupid question, I give the equally stupid answer, "one part wisdom, and two parts fact."

But back to the traditional Christian worldview that states that God is absolute and the standard of truth. Therefore, absolute laws of logic exist because they reflect the nature of an absolute God.

My worldview states that the cosmos has intrinsic objective laws. Therefore the objective laws of logic exist because they reflect the nature of an objective cosmos. Both worldviews presuppose, but my worldview presupposes a cosmos that unquestionably exists; the traditional Christian worldview presupposes God that is the "absolute and the standard of truth", which, of course, is highly debatable.

What about the idea that using logic to justify logic is "circular"? Or put another way, if asked for justification for using reason, you give a reason, then you're using a circular argument. The traditional Christian world-view uses God to justify logic, thus avoiding the circle. Or does it?

Logic comes from God —> who Christians justify the existence of using either logic or faith —> which both come from God

Also, the idea of a atheist "borrowing" Christian logic is like borrowing your cousin's 1972 Chevy Nova when you have a perfectly good Lexus. Any logic that insists 1+1+1=1 (as in the trinity), that Jesus can be 100% human and 100% God at the same time, or God can be omnipotent (create an unmovable stone) is not the kind of logic one should seek to embrace.

If we accept logic as an intrinsic objective law of the cosmos, there is no need for justification; it's simply a core understanding in which we build our worldview. Any materialist will acknowledge the existence of the intangible such as time, emotions, concepts, ideas, and logic. There is nothing spiritual, supernatural or miraculous about the intangible. Intangibles such as time and logic are intrinsic properties of our universe where others like emotions, concepts and ideas are human-created labels for processes of the mind.

Both the cosmos and the mind are amazing things to which we do not have all the answers. As long as we admit that, we won't give up looking.

Chapter 5: Argument from Ignorance / God of the Gaps

Life, as we know it, is full of mystery — from the smallest theoretical particles to what we believe to be the outer edges of our universe. What is smaller than a quark? What is outside the universe? Is there more than one universe? Are we in the first universe or the trillionth?

The cold hard fact is that we are ignorant when it comes to a complete understanding of everything. *Ignorance,* although often used as a derogatory term, is simply "not knowing". When it comes to understanding the mysteries of the universe, **we are all ignorant**. The only difference between the Nobel prize-winning astrophysicist and the local town preacher, is that the astrophysicist admits it.

There is a somewhat derogatory term called "God of the Gaps" that refers to using God to plug in the "gaps" in our scientific knowledge. What science can't currently explain, the assumption is that God must have done it, rather than accepting the fact we just don't currently have an answer. Some abuse the idea of God by treating him like a wildcard to be used where no other card seems to fit.

The *argument from ignorance* is a more general logical fallacy that asserts that a premise is true or false, just because it has not been proven to be true or false. Astrophysicist Carl Sagan describes this argument as the "Appeal to Ignorance" in Chapter 12 of his book, *The Demon-Haunted World*.

*"**Appeal to ignorance** — the claim that whatever has not been proved false must be true, and vice versa (e.g., there is no compelling evidence that UFOs are not visiting the Earth; therefore UFOs exist — and there is intelligent life elsewhere in the Universe. Or: there may be seventy kazillion other worlds, but not one is known to have the moral advancement of the Earth, so we're still central to the Universe.) This impatience with ambiguity can be criticized in the phrase: absence of evidence is not evidence of absence."*

When contemplating God's existence, theists and nontheists alike need to recognize this *appeal to ignorance*. The fact that we cannot prove God's existence in no way leads us to the logical conclusion that God does not exist. The fact that we cannot disprove God's existence in no way leads us to the logical conclusion that God does exist.

Naturalists, or those who believe that nature is all there is, and/or atheists have been accused at times of inserting a naturalistic cause out of ignorance. For example, the naturalist will explain "visions of God" by concluding they are hallucinations or the result of some meditative state. Historically speaking, this is more likely to be the case. *Never, ever*, in history has a naturalistic explanation later been proven to be an act of God. We can't say the same for the reverse.

Let's look at a few theistic arguments where God is often presumptively inserted in the premise(s) or in the conclusion.

Cosmological Argument (Kalam) - Premise #1: Everything that has a beginning has a cause. Premise #2: The universe has a beginning. Conclusion: The universe has a cause and therefore God is that cause. The fact is, if premises 1 and 2 are accepted, the conclusion is appealing to ignorance in assuming that the God of the Bible is that cause. If both premises are true, the cause is completely unknown. The fallacy is that since we cannot prove this cause is something other than God, it *must* be God.

Argument from Design (Teleological Argument) - This is the argument for God based on the evidence of apparent order, purpose, design, and direction in nature. Assuming we accepted that there did appear to be this order, purpose, design, and direction in nature, further accepting that "God did it" is simply inserting God in lieu of a "better" explanation (actually, there are many naturalistic responses to this argument).

Consciousness - We don't fully understand consciousness, so some theists will point to this as evidence of God.

The main problem with inserting God where there is currently an unknown is that it requires no research, philosophical thought, or scientific testing. It's throwing in the mental towel rather than persisting to search for an answer, even with the possibility that one may never be found. What if we never stopped assuming that sickness was really just a punishment from God? We wouldn't have hospitals; we would just have more churches — and a **lot** fewer healthy and/or living people.

Another major problem with the "God did it claim" is that the "how" question is never answered: or is it simply answered with "a miracle." For example, how did God create the universe? "He is all-powerful and can do anything," is the theist's response.

Naturalistic claims not only offer a "what" explanation, but also a "how" explanation. In fact, theists demand one — and they have every right to. If the theist is going to use miracles as the reason for how God does everything, inquiring minds are going to demand to know how those miracles work exactly — and they have every right to. The problem is, of course, a miracle, by definition, cannot be reduced to a logical explanation.

What you are not going to find in this book is a feeble attempt for me to explain the origins of the universe — or the origins of life — because it's not my goal to disprove God: nor am I qualified to give such explanations. But one of my goals is to show that God should not be used as an academic crutch — an easy way around finding real answers to hard questions.

Could the God of the Bible be the one behind the creation of the universe, the origin of life, and consciousness? It's possible. Could it be many gods? An evil God? An amoral God? A non-being powerful force? An advanced alien race? Could our physical world simply be an illusion? Perhaps everything is an illusion including other minds, and *you* are actually God who created this world and made yourself forget. Or could there be still other explanations? I don't know the right answer, and neither do you. Let's keep searching.

Chapter 6: Does the Universe Point to God?

As promised, you'll get no feeble attempt from me to explain how the universe came to be. When looking for these kinds of answers, it makes sense to defer to experts in the field of cosmology and physics, and refer to their books on the subject. For example, *A Brief History of Time* by Stephen Hawking. Hawking believes our universe was created roughly 15 billion years ago through an event known as the *Big Bang*. According to his 1988 essay, "Origin of the Universe", there was originally "nothing". But through Relativity and quantum mechanics, matter can be created out of energy in the form of particle antiparticle pairs.

In short, Hawking does not see any need for a creator, scientifically speaking. However, he acknowledges that science cannot answer the bigger question of why there is something rather than nothing. He leaves that question for "God".

Until recently, Hawking was never quite clear on his view of God. Theists and atheists have both used Hawking to support their positions. But in a 2010 interview with ABC's Diane Sawyer, Hawking made his position quite clear. *"What could define God (is thinking of God) as the embodiment of the laws of nature. However, this is not what most people would think of that God,"* Hawking said. *"They made a human-like being with whom one can have a personal relationship. When you look at the vast size of the universe and how insignificant an accidental human life is in it, that seems most impossible."*

Some may disagree with Hawking's conclusion that human life is insignificant, but I don't. In my opinion, we are not significant; we are only significant to us, we do not possess some transcendent property of "significantness".

Hawking, as bright as he may be, is not the only authority on the subject. Hawking is also not an authority on theology or God. His conclusions about God are made as a result of his study of the universe. But his conclusion is that God wasn't the "Banger" of the Big Bang.

Chapter 7: The "Fine Tuning" Argument

Perhaps the greatest atheist silencer of the 21st century is what is known as the *fine tuning* or *fine-tuned universe* argument. Ironically, this was made popular more recently by Stephen Hawking. The idea of a finely-tuned universe is quite simple, however, many people who bring this up in a religious debate make it sound really complicated by using scientific jargon to confuse people into thinking they know exactly what they are talking about, so hopefully more people will buy into their conclusion. But I digress.

Here is the argument in a nutshell: the odds that we, or anything for that matter, are here today is unimaginably small — something like one out of one with a couple hundred zeros after it. Given this extremely rare likelihood that the universe is here that and we are in it, there must be an intelligent being who "tuned" the universe to the precise settings so we can exist. The chance of us being here "by accident" is... let's just say not very good.

If you believe in God, then God did it. Case closed. He is certainly capable of creating and fine-tuning the universe. No need to look into the matter any further. But what if you do not believe in God? Then you've got a problem. You don't have an answer to a major question when your theist counterpart does. Unfortunately, you will have to either wait for science to give you a definitive answer, accept one of the many alternative theories that exist today, or come up with some of your own. Since I chose not to accept the "God did it" theory, I have a theory of my own as well as an alternate existing theory that I just expanded on a bit.

First, the "Bo Theory" (Trademark, Copyright 2011, all rights reserved). Theists want you to imagine God creating the universe at a desk (any kind of desk will do), adjusting a whole bunch of dials to the exact correct setting that allows for the universe to exist and life to exist within it. The problem with this image is that this assumes that there are "settings" that God has to follow — that he is *subordinate to*. If God were to create all the initial conditions of the universe, there would be no "adjustments" necessary — everything would be as it is upon creation.

For example, the speed of light is 299,792,458 meters per second not because it *had* to be made that way, but because it *was* made that way — assuming it was made. The perfect God of the Bible, or any "first cause" outside the universe, is not subject to any universal laws *that do not yet exist*. **What this ultimately means is that no intelligence is necessary for this creation.** Without any pre-existing laws to follow, anything goes. If there is a powerful force that is the first cause of the universe, it could be as dumb as a dodo bird and still result in the world we live in today — life and all.

Intelligence is only needed to make laws in a universe where the laws made are subject to higher fundamental laws.

Admittedly, this is not an easy concept to grasp. Everything we know about our current universe tells us that if even one of these fundamental physical constants is off by as little as a fraction of a percent, the universe cannot exist. But that is only because of the fundamental laws under which these fundamental physical constants operate. The universe works because it has to: it couldn't be otherwise.

Now for the more mainstream theory (for the record, I still prefer mine). Currently, most experts accept that the universe was created at the Big Bang. But is our universe the first attempt at a universe? Imagine the moment of the Big Bang when matter does not yet exist, but only energy. The matter ultimately created, if even created, cannot sustain an expanding universe because the "fine tuning" was not tuned very well. So, the universe collapses and tries again. Kind of like rolling the dice trying to get snake eyes, except instead of two dice you have about 10^{400} dice and you are trying to roll all ones. "Impossible!" you say. Given the constraint of time, yes, it's a statistical impossibility.

But what about a cosmos where time does not exist? If you have 2 dice, statistically you will, after about a minute, get snake eyes. If you have 10 dice, it might take you a few days to roll all ones (I am guessing here, I never tried it) but you WILL eventually get all ones. And if you had 10^{400} dice, you WILL eventually get all ones, though it will take quite a bit longer.

Now insert the *multiverse* theory and just imagine the process described above being done an infinite number of times in more than one location and/or dimension. Some "universes" make it, some don't. So far everything we know about our cosmos is an astronomically huge number — number of atoms, number of cells, number of planets, number of stars, number of galaxies, etc. Historically, we have always perceived our world to be smaller than it actually is. After all, if history is a lesson, we should not assume that this is the only "universe" in the cosmos.

Don't be wooed by what appears to be impossible odds. The world we live in today is overflowing with what would appear to be impossible odds. For example, what are the chances that you are exactly who you are, where you are now, wearing the clothes that you are wearing, *ad infinitum*? Even **greater** than the odds that the universe is here and we are in it. The lottery is difficult to win, but someone had to win it. We just happen to be those winners. Enjoy the victory.

Chapter 8: What Have We Been Up To These Last 250,000 Years?

Most paleontologists agree that humans have been on this earth for around 250,000 years or so. If this is true, it does raise two very interesting questions. One, given the progress we have made in the last 100 years alone, what have we been doing the previous 249,900 years? And two, given the population growth rate, shouldn't there be trillions of people on earth by now? Both questions actually have very logical answers.

Let's start with one of the first intellectual progresses of human kind: writing. Writing in some form or another has been around for at least 32,000 years, according to radiocarbon dating of the earliest forms of cave writings (found in the Chauvet cave in southern France). So why did it take us around 228,000 years to begin communicating through writing? The answer has to do with evolution (assuming you believe in that crazy idea). Just as we would not expect our primate friends to communicate through written language, early man didn't either. Our mental abilities to perform such tasks just were not that well developed yet. But thankfully, we have evolved.

Even in the last 32,000 years there has been relatively little progress in comparison to our last 6,000 years. Why? Evolution will only take us so far. Christian apologist, Dinesh D'Souza, suggested that around 6,000 years ago "it was like God breathed life into us." That's one theory.

But look at the progress we made in the last 30 years alone since the personal computer, or even in the last 15 years since the commercialization of the Internet. It was like Bill Gates "breathed life into us." Given inventions, discoveries, technology, wars, famine, disease, and natural disasters, our history shows that human progress is right where it should be.

As for the population growth rate, we take for granted that our hospitals and medical technology will allow us to have children who will almost always survive childbirth. It's been estimated that our ancestors of just a couple thousand years ago needed to have six children just to replace themselves. This is a tall order, even for Catholics.

Aside from the 900-year-old men in the Bible, it's generally accepted that people, on average, only lived for a fraction of the time that modern humans do. This gives our ancestors a very small window in which to have and raise children. Frankly, it's quite surprising that we are still here today.

When studying early human history, it becomes clear that evolution is responsible for our mental growth and that our mental growth is responsible for our current population size. The breath of God, as poetic as it may sound, is just not required.

Chapter 9: Common Ground and Circular Arguments

Imagine how difficult it would be for a non-*Star Trek* fan to debate the existence of God with a person who only spoke and understood Klingon. Now imagine a theist who uses the "Word of God" as the foundation of his argument while debating a philosopher who uses reason and logic as the foundation for her argument. What we end up with is a series of circular arguments that neither opponent accepts as valid. To fully understand the arguments for and against the existence of God, there needs to be common ground.

What do we mean by circular arguments? Let's say you are a theist wanting to convince your atheist buddy that God exists. You whip out your Bible, turn to John 10:30 and read where Jesus said, "I and the father are one." In your mind, it couldn't be clearer that this is proof of God. But the atheist does not accept the Bible as the Word of God, and reminds you that the reason you think the Bible is the Word of God is because it says so in the Bible.

Now, if you are the atheist and insist upon using logic and reason as the basis of argumentation, your theist friend will say that she does not accept your logic and reason as the foundation of truth and points out that you are using logic and reason to "prove" what is logical and reasonable, thus circular.

So where do you go from here?

Imagine trying to establish common ground with a Christian, a Jew, a Muslim, and an Atheist (no, this is not the beginning of an offensive joke). The Christian has his Bible, the Jew has his Torah, the Muslim has her Koran, and the atheist has her logic. It could be argued that no matter what your belief system is, we all share logic and reason as the common denominator. Let the theists insist that logic and reason come from God and let the atheist insist a naturalistic origin of logic and reason. The bottom line is that both sides can trust logic and reason — for different reasons.

However, if you hold Calvinistic beliefs that our logic and reason are tainted by "sin" — and therefore cannot be trusted — then we're back at Square One. Of course, we can also say that the formation of the Bible was guided by Satan and not the Holy Spirit: then things really get weird.

Most theists will argue the case for God on logic and reason, knowing full well that this is the most persuasive method for the non-believer. Yet very few atheists will take the time to study theology and use the Bible as the basis of argument, forgetting that logic and reason don't always work on people who believe in the supernatural and the miraculous. To engage in an intellectually- and spiritually-stimulating dialogue, one must be prepared to defend arguments from both a logical and a Biblical point of view without dismissing his or her opponent's foundation for belief. This is the common ground.

One cannot use the Bible to prove God's existence just as one cannot use the book "Harry Potter" to prove the existence of the Hogwarts School. Likewise, it's reasonable for the theist to question our logic and reason as the authoritative method for discovering truth. Be prepared to defend your position based on both reason and the Bible. And who knows, by studying both logic and the Bible, you may find yourself defending the other side.

Chapter 10: Objective Moral Values: Do They Exist?

One of the most widely-used arguments for the Christian faith is the idea of *objective moral values* (or *absolute moral values*), which has its origins in the Bible. This is the idea that our morals come from the perfectly good and moral God, and this is the basis in which we should determine what is right and wrong, or what is good or evil. It is the basis for what we "ought" to do, instead of what we feel like doing.

It has often been said that, without objective moral values, we are all free to determine what is "right." The fear, here, is that this could lead to chaos and anarchy. Without God's unchanging, absolute, moral values, we are all lost. Or are we?

Is there absolute good and evil? If the answer is yes, we need to know where this "absolute" comes from. If the answer is no, then we need to explain how something like torturing children for fun could be seen as not evil.

Let's first look at this idea of "absolute". In this case, *absolute* is referring to something independent of arbitrary standards of measurement. In other words, if something is absolutely wrong, it's wrong for everyone, in every situation, in every culture, in the past, present, and future — **no exceptions**. "Absolute" is the idea that there is only one standard of moral action and behavior and this standard is right for everyone.

However, if God is capable of changing what is absolute then by definition, absolute cannot exist. If God cannot change what is absolute, he is not omnipotent — or at least subordinate to that which is absolute. I realize that it's silly to say God cannot be omnipotent because he cannot create a circle with four corners or a married bachelor because we are asking God to *make a change* to the circle or the bachelor. In the case of absolute, no such change is requested. It just cannot be. Absolute and an omnipotent God cannot coexist. Absolute good and logic cannot coexist. Absolute good and evil do not exist.

The term *objective* is similar to absolute in the sense that it's not influenced by personal feelings, interpretations, or prejudice. Something objective is based on facts. Do you think our president is a good man? Do you think the leader of (fill in the name of enemy country of the time here) is an evil man? Depending on whom you ask, and in which country, you will get different answers.

If objective moral values existed, what "fact" are we basing them on to call them objective? On earth, fresh water freezes at 32 degrees Fahrenheit — no matter how people personally feel about the matter. That is a fact. However, this notion of good and evil is subjective. Objective good and evil do not exist.

Okay, so how can we possibly say that torturing children for fun is not ALWAYS bad (or evil)? Unlike temperature, there are no logical, mathematical, or scientific facts involved. You and I may both think something is evil and wrong, but we are just two minds in a world of billions. It's pure arrogance to think that everyone who does not think the way we do is wrong or evil. Perhaps somewhere in the world — in the past, present, or future — a tribe might happily "torture" (a subjective word) children (another subjective word) as a right of passage to prepare them for adulthood. In other words, the unknown "greater good" is always a possibility.

But what about Hitler? Or the terrorists of 9/11? Or Jeffrey Dahmer (the guy who murdered people and ate them)? The Catholic Church actually honored Hitler on his birthday each year, the "terrorists" believed they were doing the work of Allah for the greater good, and Jeffrey Dahmer was just really hungry. We fail to see good and evil as subjective because we fail to take into consideration cultural and societal norms. But most of all, we fail to understand our fellow humans. It is much easier for us to make moral judgments based on *our* morals rather than accept the idea that the line separating good and evil is not as clear as we once thought.

In Matthew 7:18, Jesus himself said, *"A good tree cannot bear bad fruit, and a bad tree cannot bear good fruit."* Does this apply to God as well? How could an existence created by a pure good God result in good AND evil? Freewill doesn't cut it, because evil would still need to exist for us to be able to choose.

Some may say that evil is simply the absence of good, like cold is the absence of heat. To me, that is a pretty weak definition. The "absence of good" is eating a salad without delicious dressing. The "absence of good" is evident in my musical talent. The absence of good is not evil — at least nothing like how we define evil.

Besides, cold is *not* the absence of heat. Temperature is scientifically measured by the speed of molecules and cold is a subjective word that we use to describe matter with slow moving molecules. Unlike temperature, good and evil have no such measurable scale — they are purely subjective.

Word games like this provide apparent solutions to real philosophical problems. Of course, good cannot exist without evil, hot without cold, up without down, dark without light. It is quite simply the nature of our universe. These ideas are meaningless without their opposite.

Goodness is said to come from God as a reflection of his nature. We know God primarily through the Bible. It is clear that in the Bible, God commands many things that any moral person today would find revolting. It has been argued in God's defense that he did these things in a different time, to an "evil" people, for reasons we cannot understand. Absolute morality, by definition, is unchanging, so there should be no reason God's actions back then were morally acceptable when today they are not. It is hard to imagine what crime these millions of slaughtered and drowned men, women, children, animals — and all other forms of life —committed to be deserving of God's wrath. And perhaps, there are reasons beyond our understanding for God's extreme genocidal actions. But if that is the case, we have NO way of knowing what absolute morality is because of this missing "greater good" that we are apparently too feeble-minded to understand. To clarify, I will rephrase this as a logical argument:

Premise 1) God appears take actions that appear extreme or cruel based on today's moral standards

Premise 2) God must be all good and perfectly just

Premise 3) We are incapable of understanding God's reasons for taking the actions he did as written in the Bible

Conclusion) Therefore, deriving moral values from Biblical verses based on the reported actions of God is unreasonable

This is even working under the assumption that the Bible is the absolute "Word of God".

What about the moral code "written in our hearts"? (2 Corinthians 3:2) If God is the ultimate source of morality, and it's clear that we cannot determine this morality from the Bible, then God must reveal this perfect morality to us in other ways, primarily through our hearts. Would this mean then that some people have this code and others don't? How about the mentally ill who are unable to determine right from wrong? What's wrong with their hearts? What if a Christian gets the heart of an atheist in a transplant? Biologically, how is the code even written?

Insisting that God writes the moral code in our hearts is scientifically, logically, and spiritually equivalent to saying lightening strikes when God is angry. But perhaps the use of the word "heart" is meant as more of a figure of speech. If we were born with any sense of morality, it's very likely a result of our biological evolution that serves as a mechanism to help the survival of our species.

If God were the ultimate source of good — and what is right — one would think that all those who "know God" would have the same sense of what is good and right. The underlying accusation is that those who really know God know what is good and they know what is evil. Everyone else is simply mistaken. But obviously that is not the case. Theists, even Christians, disagree widely on many issues including homosexuality, divorce, abortion, use of contraceptives, and much more. This is usually written off as misinterpreting God's word, rationalization, human imperfection — or even being misled by Satan.

Given our state of imperfection and human misunderstanding, why insist that morals must be absolute or objective if they are always up to subjective interpretation anyway? Some fear that without a belief in God, there is no ultimate judge and therefore no reason to live a moral life that is conducive to growth, prosperity, and happiness. However, imagine for a moment that God did write moral code in our hearts: he would write this code whether we believe in him or not, so belief in God would have no effect on our behavior, so there is nothing to worry about.

If, however, our behavior is governed by the fear of God's wrath (punishment in this life or the next), then we should be able to empirically prove that non-believers in God display less moral behavior than their theist counterparts. But we can't. The idea that without a divine babysitter, we would have sex with animals in the streets, become crack-heads, murder everyone who upsets us, and drive 65 in a 55mph zone, is not only ridiculous, but offensive — to me and anyone else like me, who takes full responsibility for his or her moral choices.

What if there is no Heaven or Hell? Does that mean this life has no consequences? Absolutely not. We all are fully aware that this life has consequences that are directly tied to our behaviors and actions. If we cheat on our spouse, we destroy that relationship. If we murder someone, we spend our lives incarcerated — or at least in fear of incarceration. If we lie, we lose the trust of our loved ones and peers.

The big "crime" that goes unpunished in this life is not worshiping God (the first four commandments). This is perhaps why theists generally despise the thought of no eternal punishment and cherish the idea of eternal reward. In my view, there is no question that eternal punishment and reward are strong motivators — especially for children — but morality also consists of doing the right things for the right reasons. Behaving well to avoid God's wrath is like returning a lost wallet because you are hoping for a large cash reward.

So where does our morality come from? Morality is defined as the *conformity to the rules of conduct*. Without conformity, we would not be able to survive, and certainly not prosper as a species. It may sound overly simple, but *morality is nothing more than living a life according to some form of the Golden Rule*. The idea of "doing to others only what you would want them to do to you" can be found in many ancient writings — many of which predate the Bible.

Remember back to when you were a child learning to play with others? You grabbed toys away from others, you pushed others, you made fun of others — you basically acted *immorally*. You did all this guilt free with no regret until others starting doing the same thing to you. It was then that you realized what you instinctively felt like doing is not the same as what you "ought" to do.

Let's fast-forward many years to adulthood. You have lived your life with empathy and are capable of understanding the feelings — both positive and negative — of others as a result of experiencing your own feelings. When we see people suffer it's like we are suffering. We want to help — not by some divine command or some mystical force — but by our natural emotional response due to a lifetime of conditioning. When it comes to surviving and thriving, love is more conducive than hate. It really is that simple.

There is no objective good and there is no objective evil. These are just ideas that we use to define how we feel about something, and not everyone has to agree. Love is good for most, but to the woman scorned, love is Hell. The concepts of right and wrong are doing what we perceive to be good, and doing what we perceive to be evil. Right and wrong are purely subjective.

Morality is a byproduct of our actions and the consequences of living a life according to some form of the Golden Rule. I know this is a hard pill to swallow, especially for theists. However, if every human had the same sense of right and wrong, the world would be a very different place than it is today.

Chapter 11: Dying for the Faith

Christian tradition maintains that eleven of the twelve disciples of Jesus were martyred for their faith (it's believed that John, the disciple to whom the Gospel of John and the Book of Revelation are attributed, died of old age). While scripture only mentions how James gave his life (Acts 12:2), later Christian writings based on oral tradition tell stories of how the ten other disciples eventually died for the faith.

While there is very little historical evidence of this, it's believed that all 12 disciples were at least willing to die for their beliefs. It is often argued by Christians, "Why would anyone be willing to die for something they knew was a lie?" So this appears to be a pretty solid argument for the story of Christianity — given the resolve of the disciples.

Without a time machine, none of us can know for sure how much of this tradition is true versus how much is legend. But let's assume that eleven of the twelve disciples *did* actually end up giving their lives for the faith. Based on this assumption, let's accept this as evidence for the story of Christianity, or more specifically, the foundational event of Christianity — the resurrection of Jesus.

Okay, so let's look again at how the most common form of this argument is phrased: "Why would anyone be willing to die for something they knew was a lie?" I guess if someone were insisting that all the followers of Jesus were spreading a known lie, then that would be a reasonable response. But what if the disciples, like many Christians today, really just *believed* in the resurrection of Jesus? We have many writings from the first few centuries with stories of Christian martyrs who lived many generations after Jesus. The martyrs gave their lives for the faith not because they had some inside information; but because they simply had *very strong beliefs*.

The general assumption here is that if someone is willing to give his or her life for something, it is evidence of that "something" having truth. But we know that virtually all religions have their martyrs (think 9/11). And we know that *all* the underlying beliefs cannot be true, since *all* religions cannot be true at the same time.

Here is another example: Do you remember the "Heaven's Gate" cult? In March, 1997, 39 people killed themselves because they held a firm belief that they were just "giving up their physical bodies" so that their souls could hitch a ride on a spaceship following a comet. Possible? Sure. Probable? Highly doubtful. While technically not martyrs, the Heaven's Gate clan gave their lives for a belief based on a faith that most of us can agree is almost certainly not true.

Martyrdom simply requires belief, not truth.

Chapter 12: Creationism, Evolution, and Intelligent Design

How did we get here? Since we can't go back in time to find out, we can either believe in one of the hundreds of creation stories that have been passed down from generation to generation, we can use science to help us find the answer, or we can use a little of both. Respectively, these are the basic ideas of *Creationism*, *Evolution*, and *Intelligent Design*.

Creationism is the idea that we already know how the world began and how we came to be since it's written in the Bible. God did it. It would seem simple enough, yet there are as many varieties of creationism as there are holes in the theory itself. Some creationists insist the universe is no older than 6,000 years, some insist God created every species in their existing form we see today. But all creationists insist that hundreds of years of scientific empirical evidence as well as scientific proof about the nature of universe, are just dead wrong. Why? Despite what you may think, it's not because "God said otherwise," but rather it's *their interpretation* of the passages in the book of Genesis that forces them to deny any science that contradicts their interpretation. So in reality, it's not the "Word of God" against fallible human scientists; it's the very fallible creationist's literal interpretation of the Bible against widely accepted scientific facts.

Evolution, in the context of this article, refers to the biological changes of living organisms from the first signs of life on earth to the present day. This is more commonly known as the *"Theory of Evolution"*. Unlike my theory that people with bad body odor are somehow attracted to me in crowded places, a *scientific theory* is a well-substantiated explanation of some aspect of the natural world that can incorporate facts, laws, inferences, and tested hypotheses. According to the *National Academy of Sciences*, evolution is one of the strongest and most useful scientific theories we have.

The idea of evolution has been around long before Charles Darwin, even though he is the man most associated with the theory of evolution. In fact, Darwin's grandfather was a proponent of the theory, as were many people before and after him. Charles Darwin actually introduced the idea of *natural selection* in the mid 1800s, which is an explanation as to *how* evolution occurs.

The idea in its original form did not take hold right away. It wasn't until the years 1936 to 1947 that scientists of many specific fields came to agreement on what is known as the *(modern) evolutionary synthesis*, which has been accepted by nearly all working biologists. However, evolution is not without its critics. Although many theists today accept the theory of evolution, many do not agree on *how exactly* evolution occurs. *Theistic evolutionists* and *intelligent design proponents* agree that evolution occurs, but maintain that God is the ultimate force behind evolution. How much God has to do with evolution varies among believers. Some believe that God initiated the process with a single miracle and he has allowed natural processes to guide it from there. Some believe that God not only initiated the process, but continually guides the process, usually in place of natural selection. But this involvement of God is, and can only be, a faith-based claim.

It seems as if the idea that we evolved from a more primitive life form is not just unbelievable to many people, but *horrifying* as well. Although evolution states that we share a common ancestor with apes, the evolution deniers like to say that they don't believe that they evolved from "pond scum" or something equally as vile. I find this argument, if one can call it that, quite amusing since the alternative is that God made us from dirt and blew life into our noses (Genesis 2:7). Why does the idea that we evolved make us any less special? That fact that my great ancestor might have been some kind of fungus does not make my life worthless. It's not where you come from; it's where you're headed that matters most.

So what is true? Creationism, evolution, or some form of intelligent design? The intelligent design folks do make some convincing arguments to the lay person (like me), but none that have been taken seriously by the scientific community. I think intelligent design proponents have too little faith in the power of the God in which they believe. Wouldn't a perfect God create the universe in one perfect moment with all the rules set in place, without requiring his constant intervention and tinkering? If God were a watchmaker, he would make the kind of watch that you don't have to wind up everyday. But of course, who am I to pretend to know the mind of God?

As for creationism, as open-minded as I like to think I am, I just cannot see any truth to creationism. Here is just one of the many reasons why: for one to deny evolution, he or she must deny the essence of scientific study. If one of the strongest and most useful scientific theories we have is completely wrong, it would reason that every scientific theory we hold as true today could easily be just as wrong, since the scientific methods used must be seriously flawed.

Unlike the Genesis account that provides nothing more than a fascinating look into the minds of iron-age thinking, the theory of evolution helps to explain the emergence of new infectious diseases as well as the development of antibiotic resistance in bacteria — real world explanations that have helped us save countless lives. And as geneticist and evolutionist Theodosius Dobzhansky wrote in 1973, *"Nothing in biology makes sense except in the light of evolution."*

Countless scientists in the areas of genetics, biochemistry, neurobiology, physiology, ecology — and other biological disciplines — continually study evolution. These people spend their lives studying *how* evolution occurs fully accepting that is *does* occur just as they accept that the earth rotates around the sun. The creationist simply refers to a very old book that suggests, "God did it."

Perhaps it's my lack of faith, or maybe it's Satan deceiving me, but I just cannot ignore the facts of evolution (in science, a fact is an observation that has been repeatedly confirmed and for all practical purposes is accepted as true). If you or anyone you know suffers from creationism, I urge you to download the free booklet from the National Academy of Sciences entitled *Science and Creationism: A View from the National Academy of Sciences, Second Edition* available at http://www.nap.edu.

Although I love a good challenge to commonly held beliefs, I don't think I can seriously consider the possibility of the Genesis account representing an historical event and a scientific fact. The intelligent design vs. natural selection debate is certainly more interesting, I'll admit. But science already has significant evidence leading to the purely naturalistic creation of life.

But in the spirit of open-mindedness, I'll admit that science, by definition, can say nothing about the idea of whether God started the whole process or not.

Chapter 13: Is Religion Child Abuse?

I loved my parents very much, yet they still brought me up with some twisted beliefs. My mom was a huge UFO fan and used to talk about aliens all the time like they were part of our society. In fact, I couldn't sleep alone with the lights off until my 20s, in fear that these aliens would abduct me and stick probes in inappropriate places (yes, somehow I reasoned that illumination prevented alien abduction). My father believed that four packs of cigarettes and a half bottle of Seagram's Seven every day was the best way to live life, arguing, "Were all going to die eventually anyway!"

I am pretty sure I'm not the only one raised with some erroneous, strange, and sometimes destructive beliefs. Do religious beliefs fall into this category? Some of the new atheists argue that raising a child with religious teachings is not just a form of brainwashing, but they go as far as to call it child abuse. Should kids not be taught religion? And what harm, if any, are these beliefs causing children?

I was raised Catholic and sent to Sunday school from third grade until my confirmation in the eighth grade. No, I did not have a choice — at least to the extent that any child actually has a choice in these kinds of matters. I was taught and believed many of the theistic ideas, as well as the more specific theological ideas held by Catholics. In retrospect, the only "harm" it did me was taking away about an hour of TV watching each week. As a result of my religious studies, I remember participating in many community events, helping out at old-age homes (that is, where the people in the homes are old, not the homes themselves), organizing charity events, and much more.

While I cannot assume that every religious upbringing was as harmless as mine, I think it's safe to say that starting religious education at a young age is not the problem; when some radical form of religion is mixed with politics, then that's a different story.

The real issue is refusing to take control over our own lives and blaming our parents, teachers — even society — for our problems. Although my father professed his life philosophy to me many times, I knew it was not the way I wanted to live my life. Many years later, I questioned the idea that alien abduction was a common event and realized that my mom was just watching way too many sci-fi movies.

I once read a powerful book where the author encouraged us to question all of our beliefs and frequently reevaluate them to see if they still make sense to us at different stages in our lives. This is great advice. The book was titled, *"Year To Success"* by Bo Bennett (shameless plug).

The problem is not religious instruction; it's raising kids with any false or destructive belief. The solution is to encourage both children and adults to frequently question their beliefs. Of course, if you're counting on the threat of Hell to keep your kids in line, then forget everything I just said.

I know parents will want their children to adopt the same beliefs as they have. If you believe something is true, why wouldn't you want your children to know that truth? In an ideal world, I would love to see a required "World Religions" course in schools that provides an introduction to the many religions practiced today all over the world. I would also like to see parents explain to their children that their religion, or lack of religion, is *their belief* and encourage their children to challenge this belief by asking questions. And most importantly, I would hope that all parents would allow their children to adopt their own beliefs without fear of persecution or worry of parental disappointment.

While they may not technically be responsible for child abuse, intolerant parents who refuse to extend the "freedom of religion" right to their children are walking the line.

Chapter 14: It's a Miracle!

The word "miracle" has become so watered down in our culture that we even associate it with artery-clogging condiments used by people too cheap to spend an extra 30 cents on *Hellmann's Real Mayonnaise*. When the underdog emerges victorious during a sporting event, we call it a "miracle". We call it a "miracle" when a good-looking kid is the offspring of two not-so-attractive parents. From a high-fat sandwich spread to cute kids, the word "miracle" has become synonymous with everyday events. But this isn't the kind of miracle that serves as the foundation of Christianity — or of most religions for that matter.

The Biblical kind of miracle I will define as *an intervention of the divine as made evident by the violation of all known natural laws* is the kind of miracle that's the subject of this chapter. I do not believe, nor do I think anyone should insist that a mere apparent violation of natural law constitutes a miracle. Modern science has been around for just a few hundred years out of our roughly 250,000-year existence. How can we possibly be so arrogant as to assume that we know all of the laws of nature? Today we are just beginning to understand particle and quantum physics and how these new areas just might change the way we see reality. Take for example the common "miracle" of spontaneous cancer remission. People seem really amazed that doctors can't explain why this happens. Out of the last five times I went to the doctor for common aliments, three of those times my doctor didn't have a clue as to what was wrong with me. The ignorance of the "professional" community doesn't constitute a miracle; it just verifies their ignorance.

So if I insist that a miracle requires the intervention of the divine, how in the world can one prove this intervention? Well, they can't. But they can *suggest evidence* for divine intervention. Let's go back to our example of spontaneous cancer remission. If a faithful believer of God prays many times a day for her cancer to be gone, then it goes away overnight, it certainly would appear to suggest divine intervention. But what about all those documented cases where non-believers report spontaneous cancer remission? Now we have evidence that this unexplained phenomenon appears to be unrelated to the divine.

We hear much more about the spontaneous cancer remissions attributed to God because we love hearing stories about miracles and the media knows it. The televangelists also love to show us little old ladies throwing away their walkers thanks to the power of God. But what they don't want us to know is that many older people, who use walkers, canes, and even wheelchairs, do not require them. They are using them to help prevent injury. Connecting an unexplained event to the deliberate will of God is as impossible as the miracle itself.

What kinds of miracles exist today? Look on the Internet and you see them all over the place. We see healings credited to God, Hindu statues dripping milk, guru *Sathya Sai Baba's* "miracles" (who claims to be born of a virgin) believed by hundreds of thousands of people, and the list goes on.

But each and every one of these stories can better be explained by the power of the mind (as experienced by the placebo effect), cheap parlor tricks, coincidences, statistical necessities (i.e. someone has to the win the lottery), and charlatans taking advantage of a person's gullibility and a desire for the miraculous. When was the last time we witnessed a resurrection (resurrection, not resuscitation), the sun "stopping" in the middle of the sky, wives turning into pillars of salt, angels slaughtering first-born children, talking donkeys (outside of the movie *Shrek*), seas parting, and the hundreds of other "holy crap" types of miracles that we read about in the Bible?

Let's go back a couple of thousand years. Imagine you are living in a time when there was no science as we know it today. No understanding of biology, cosmology, disease, the laws of nature, and the laws of physics. It was a common belief that either the God, or many gods, were responsible for pretty much everything. If you did experience something outside your normal everyday empirical observation, such as an eclipse, volcano eruption, drought, or disease, it was just God (or the gods) interfering in the world. If you were to hear stories of God turning people into salt pillars, making donkeys talk, or resurrecting the dead after three days, it would not go against your common knowledge and your understanding of the universe because *you didn't have today's common knowledge and understanding of the universe*. You would have simply accepted these stories as fact back then as easily as you would accept the discovery of a new species of butterfly as fact today.

If you accept the miraculous as a valid explanation for the unknown, where do you draw the line? Do you believe in *all* the miracle stories in the Bible, or just in some of them? How about the miracle stories in many early Christian writings that did not make it into the Bible? How about the countless people who have claimed and do claim to be the second coming of Jesus?

If you are like the majority of Christians, you believe in some miracles in the Bible and not in others. You might explain this by saying you use logic or a more reasonable interpretation of the scripture to determine what miracle stories are just symbolic. However, logic and reason are outside the realm of the miraculous — miracles are neither reasonable nor logical.

Ask yourself, on what basis do you reject some Biblical miracles and accept others?

Now let's look at the probability of miracles occurring. Given probable possible explanations of an event, are miracles always the least probable possible explanation? Well, *it depends on what you are using for the basis of your comparison.* We can all agree that alleged miracles are extremely rare compared to the number of events that can be explained. For example, in the past 3,000 years, based on an estimated 1,000 virgin birth claims and 25 billion people born, there is a .000004% chance that someone will seriously claim to be born of a virgin (ignoring the validity of the claim for now).

So if we ask the question, "Is it less likely that Jesus was born of a virgin than through sexual intercourse?" compared to the other 24,999,998,999 regular births, **YES**, the virgin birth miracle is certainly less likely. But if we accept the idea that Jesus was born of a virgin, now we ask the question, "Is it less likely that the virgin birth of Jesus was a miracle than the virgin birth being a result of a form of asexual reproduction found in females, where growth and development of embryos occurs without fertilization by a male (parthenogenesis)?" Since there are no known cases of human births through parthenogenesis — and no serious claims for that matter — the option of a miracle is on equal ground.

What about the resurrection of Jesus? Given the assumption that only one in the last 25 billion people to have walked this earth is claimed to be resurrected from the dead, is it more likely that the resurrection of Jesus was a symbolic representation of Christian theology than a historical event? YES, it is extremely more likely. But, if one were to accept the idea that Jesus did come back from the dead after three days, since there are no natural resurrections to compare this to, a miracle becomes an option of reasonable probability. As you can see, many of religion's miraculous claims are indeed the least probable possible explanation. That is, of course, assuming you don't throw all logic completely out the window.

Although science can easily disprove many alleged modern-day miracles, **science can never prove miracles**. Accepting the unexplained as a miracle is an act of faith because claiming to know that God suspended the laws of the universe can only be done through faith. In many cases, accepting the miraculous requires a complete disregard of logic and statistical probabilities along with an enormous leap of faith.

Our world consists of many unexplained phenomenon and we should certainly give credit where credit is due. But to ignore the "miracle" that is within each of us, is to deny the entire human race the possibility that the human mind just might be the source behind much of what we cannot explain.

Chapter 15: Freewill and Determinism

A moment ago, I chose to write about this subject. I feel as if I made that choice freely. But did I really make this choice freely, or was it inevitable based on an almost infinite series of prior causes and events? In other words, could I have possibly made any other choice given my genetics, upbringing, education, knowledge, past choices and thoughts? If the answer's yes, that's *freewill*. If the answer's no, that's *determinism*.

This philosophical debate has been going strong since the ancient Greek philosopher *Leucippus* produced the earliest known view on the debate roughly 2500 years ago.

Although most contemporary philosophers and scientists believe we do possess some form of freewill, the extent of that freewill is a source of continual study and debate. And the idea that we might not be as "freewilled" as we thought can have significant implications on religion, as we will see.

The idea of determinism is quite scary. Imagine that anything and everything you do has been predetermined and you are powerless to create your own destiny. You may think you are in the driver's seat, but every single choice you make you *had* to make — it couldn't be any other way.

But some people like the idea of being a passenger in the car of life, as long as God is the driver. The big question is: can you tell God to stop the car and get out if you wanted to? If you can't, freewill doesn't exist, and you are nothing more than God's puppet and can no more make moral choices than your mailbox can. Of course, this means that you cannot be held morally responsible for your actions, or your beliefs. It would be wrong for God to judge you in Heaven.

Without freewill, the whole idea of personal responsibility and salvation collapses.

But worry not. God is said to have given us the gift of freewill. The ironic part is, as author and journalist Christopher Hitchens frequently points out, we have no choice but to accept it. Or do we?

Even if freewill does exist, we have significant empirical evidence, which shows that much of who we are, the decisions we make, and the beliefs we hold are either influenced, or in some cases, predetermined — by factors outside of our control. Some of these factors include genetics, brain activity/defects caused by physical trauma, family environment, hormones, education/ignorance, peers, drugs and alcohol, luck and/or chance, and others. Some of these influences, especially when combined with others, are so powerful, that "free choice" in this case would be like the "free choice" you have to stop eating for several days. It's possible, but painful, and some might even suggest against nature.

While it may not be classical determinism, many people, perhaps most of us, can attribute our actions, behaviors, and beliefs to a series of highly-influential past events. Which leads to the question: would you treat people any differently if you knew that it was *extremely difficult* for them to be any other way than they are now? Do you think God would?

Let's assume that there is a perfectly just God who judges us at the time of our death and allows us into a wonderful place called Heaven if we believed in him at the time of our death. Take two people, both with freewill and both who did not believe — myself and St. Paul. Wouldn't St. Paul have an advantage since Jesus appeared to him even though Paul didn't ask for it? That sucks for me who doesn't even get an appearance by him on my burnt piece of toast. I can really use that kind of revelation to assure my ticket into Heaven.

In this case, the influential factor would be "divine influence". Paul still has the freewill to deny Jesus, but given that Jesus has appeared to him and said "I am Jesus, whom you are persecuting..." (Acts 9:5), his freewill has been influenced quite a bit, to say the least.

When we live our lives assuming pure freewill, we ignore the circumstances which led a fellow human to their current situation and feel hostility toward them for their "poor" choices rather than feel empathy and understanding. But when we recognize that there are influential and even deterministic forces at work, we see people in a whole new light. No longer are people simply evil. They are just people who happen to do "bad" things to whom we can offer words of encouragement and support while helping them to overcome the negative forces working against them.

Do you have freewill? Prove it and make the choice to change your attitude towards others.

Of course, that's really not proof since you could have been predetermined to do this anyway.

PART III: BELIEF

Chapter 16: Belief and Christianity

Why do we believe what we believe, and most importantly, do we really have a choice in the matter? The latter is a question of extreme importance, since Christian faith hinges on *belief*—the belief that Jesus is your savior, that Jesus physically (bodily) was raised from the dead, and that Jesus is God. There is a major difference between just *saying* you believe and *truly believing*, and don't try to fake it because any omniscient God would certainly know the difference. But should an omnibenevolent and perfectly just God sentence you to eternal suffering and torment as a result of deterministic forces outside of your control? Of course not.

As children we believe just about anything our parents tell us. They tell us that a change-dispensing fairy sneaks into our rooms at night and leaves money under our pillows in exchange for our fallen teeth. They tell us that a super-sized rabbit with a sugar addiction breaks into our house once a year and leaves baskets of candy, which, ironically, leads to more tooth fairy encounters. They tell us of an old man in the sky with a white beard who always watches over us and an underground-dwelling red demon with a pitchfork who tries to temp us to do bad things. We believe these things right away because we lack sufficient contrary evidence and/or information as well as the ability for more advanced reasoning that develops with age. Whether you were raised Christian or as an atheist, you need to question what you were taught as a child and see if it still makes sense to the adult you.

In the simplest terms, we can say that our beliefs are formed by *information we receive*. Depending on that information, our beliefs can be very different. Take for example two twin boys separated at birth. One boy lives with his Christian mother and the other with his Jewish father. The boy raised Christian believes in Santa Claus with all of his heart yet the boy raised Jewish sees Santa as an obvious fictional character. The little boys did not choose their beliefs, they did not even choose the information to which they were exposed, they simply were products of their environment. Furthermore, based on the information to which they were exposed, it would be unreasonable to expect them to believe anything different.

However, we are not children. We are big boys and girls who are capable of making our own choices and decisions. But can we really choose to believe or disbelieve something at will? We can certainly choose the information to which we are exposed and consume. While this information does play an important role in forming our belief system, it's not always enough to form a belief. True belief turns out to be much more deterministic than the simple choices we make. It is very much like choosing our profession. What we do for a living is highly influenced by our upbringing, education, financial background, natural abilities, talents, society, chance, and dare I say, luck. While it's possible for a 5-foot-3-inch guy to become a professional basketball player (Muggsy Bogues) or a tone-def Chinese guy to become an international musical sensation (William Hung), it's extremely unlikely. And while it's possible for a Jewish Rabbi to believe in Nazism or any adult of average intelligence to believe in Leprechauns, it's extremely unlikely.

You can experiment with this idea yourself by trying to make yourself believe something you currently do not believe. Start by seeking information that supports your desired new belief. For example, if you currently think climate change is a serious problem, then you might start with the book, *Climate Confusion*, by Roy W. Spencer to help you understand the other side of the argument. If you believe that man really walked on the moon, you might want to Google, "moon landing hoax" and watch Buzz Aldrin punch a skeptic in the face. Or if you consider yourself an atheist, you might try reading a Christian book or two on the evidence of the resurrection. With this new understanding, you will almost certainly find yourself more open to the idea that your former beliefs may not be 100% correct. You might even find that your beliefs have changed. But sometimes, no matter how much exploration you do, or how badly you want to change your belief, you just can't.

There is a difference between *acceptance* and *justified belief*, which can best be explained though a personal example. I *accept* climate change as a real problem that needs to be addressed. I accept this because the evidence I have been exposed to leads me in that direction. I wouldn't say I *believe* that climate change is a real problem because I cannot honestly say that I have evaluated the evidence for and against the issue to form a *justified belief*. In a way, one can say that I accept climate change out of ignorance, and I would agree. There are far too many issues in this world to form a justified belief on all of them. This is where acceptance and opinions come in. But if there is any issue that is deserving of our attention, it's religion.

So back to the question, is it just to be judged based on what we believe? Does God want us to keep far away from any information that would put doubt in our minds? And if we, as adults, *cannot* believe in all the claims of Christianity after evaluating the arguments and information, are we to blame? After all, was it not God who gave us our reason, our intellect, and our quest for truth? This poses a major problem for any faith where the promise of salvation and eternal paradise is based on factors outside of our control — at least when a perfectly good and just God is the judge. If belief in the supernatural is the way to eternal paradise, then knowledge, logic, and reason are not gifts; they are curses.

Chapter 17: Crazy or a Really Faithful Christian?

I read a true story about a man named John List who lost his job and was worried that being forced to move to a low-income neighborhood would cause his children to abandon Christ and stray from religion. In order to "save their souls," on November 9, 1971, he "sent them to Heaven" early by shooting his own children to death. While he was at it, he took out his wife and mother as well. He then fled the scene and remained a fugitive for 18 years until he was captured in 1989. Given his religious justification, one has to ask, was this guy crazy or just a really faithful Christian?

As a Christian, you most likely believe in Hell as Jesus himself warns against it in Mark 9:43-48 — the gory scene where Jesus appears to be describing the prequel to the movie *Saw*. If you believe in Hell, you most likely will agree that it's the worst place imaginable. In fact, Rev 14:10-11 does a hell of a good job describing the place: *"He shall be tormented with fire and brimstone...the smoke of their torment ascended up forever and ever: and they have no rest day or night."* You also most likely believe that those who reject Christ as their savior will go to Hell as according to 1 Thessalonians 1:8-9, *"He will punish those who do not know God and do not obey the gospel of our Lord Jesus. They will be punished with **everlasting destruction** and shut out from the presence of the Lord and from the majesty of his power."* So let's recap:

- You believe in Hell
- You believe that Hell is the worst place imaginable
- You believe that souls sent there suffer for eternity
- You believe those who reject Christ as their savior go to Hell

With an eternal existence, life on this earth is no more than a speck in time. So why would any sane and kind person NOT do *anything* to save the souls of loved ones by sending them to Heaven early? Why stop there? Why risk allowing *any* children to grow up and reject Christ? Why not send *all current believers* to Heaven right away before they get their hands on my book and change their minds? Why ever risk having children in the first place since they might grow up to reject Christ? Given our eternal existence, what does it really matter anyway if our mortal lives are cut short by a few dozen earth years? Isn't Heaven, or perhaps more importantly, the avoidance of Hell worth it?

You can see the big problem here. Perhaps the least "Christian-like" act can be easily Biblically justified to be the most "Christian-like". After all, the killings are not necessarily really murder; it's more like killing in the name of God, which has been justified countless times before. Yet it's obvious that almost all Christians would not even think of doing such a horrible thing (horrible by our own standards of course). So why do *we* allow our loved ones, and others, to live long enough to reject Christ?

The answer for me is simple. I don't believe in Hell. Neither do a good number of Christians. Some Christians think Hell exists but don't believe that Hell is really that terrible of a place; kind of like being stuck in a Kmart for all eternity — you can tolerate it, but you would prefer not to. Some Christians don't buy into the "eternity" bit because they can't imagine any crime that would justify that kind of torment, or any loving God that would allow for such a punishment. And some Christians believe that there are other ways to avoid Hell. Note that although all these beliefs seem reasonable, some can be justified by alternative (dare I say contradicting?) passages in scripture while others have no Biblical basis whatsoever.

Back to the opening question: Was this guy John List crazy or just a really faithful Christian? If he were simply following what appears to be a very clear, non-extremist interpretation of the Bible's view on Hell, his conclusion, although unthinkable by our standards, was not only logical, but sacrificial. God sacrificed just one child; this guy sacrificed three (plus a wife and a mother) to ensure them their place in Heaven. Crazy? **Yes.** In my opinion, this guy was crazy. He was a psycho, wacko, and nut job all rolled up into one. His craziness, combined with his firm belief in the "Word of God" and the idea of immortal existence led him to commit this heinous crime. Human sacrifice *is murder* (in the case of God sacrificing Jesus I guess it's more like martyrdom, since they are one). The formula is quite simple, yet extremely toxic... like Diet Coke, Mentos, and a kid with a video camera:

Belief that the Bible is the "Word of God" + Immortality/ Resurrection + Crazy = DISASTER.

We really cannot blame the Bible for life everlasting because if the Bible is indeed the Word of God, then it's the Word of God — true is true. If we are all immortal we are immortal. And for as long as there will be people, there will be crazy. What if we all just acknowledged that possility that the Bible *might just possibly* be the words of fallible man and *just maybe* when we die, we cease to exist? If everyone were open to these possibilities, then perhaps we would see a lot less disaster, and a lot fewer horrifying headlines.

Chapter 18: 'Cause I Gotta Have Faith

The 80's pop icon, George Michael, tells us, while wearing his painted on jeans, that we gotta have faith-a-faith-a-faith.

Similarly, Jesus told us the same thing about 2000 years earlier in a less musical way, most likely wearing something a little more loose-fitting. What does faith mean today? What did Jesus and other writers of scripture mean by "faith" and how do we get it?

Today, faith means *believing in something that does not rest on logical proof or material evidence.* This is like a teacher telling all her new students that she has *faith* that they will all do an amazing job this year. The teacher has no evidence to support this and certainly no proof — it's more of an affirmation or form of positive thinking. If I were to say that I have faith that my wife will remember to meet me somewhere, I am using the term incorrectly because I have 15 years of mental data that tells me she never stood me up before. This data is the material evidence required change faith into a *justified belief.* While *Biblical faith* is similar to the modern definition of faith, for many believers, it has its differences.

The author of Hebrews 11:1 (NIV) tells us that faith is "being sure of what we hope for and certain of what we do not see." This Biblical definition is similar to today's definition of faith, but the big difference is that this definition of faith *leaves no room for doubt.* To use my earlier examples, a teacher *hopes* her students will do amazing work, and if she is a good actress, will project confidence and speak words to match her hope, but inside she knows through reason and past experiences that there will be kids who don't do well. We can get all literal on this and say that we have "faith in oxygen" because we hope for it to be there and we are certain it is, although we cannot see it. But it's clear that "what we do not see" refers to today's modern definition of faith where proof or evidence is lacking.

Is this kind of Biblical faith even possible? To the non-believer, it doesn't seem possible. I can't think of anything in which I am *certain* about that is not backed up by either proof or at least a reasonable amount of evidence. As a non-believer, I do often use faith, but in the modern sense where doubt is always present whenever there is lack of evidence and/or proof. But many believers claim they do have this kind of faith and many martyrs have proved it. So how does one get this level of faith? Some have suggested that this level of faith can only come from God (Ephesians 2:8-9, Heb 12:2), but if that were true, then God chooses who believes or not, and non-believers, such as myself, cannot be judged based on faith alone. Some have suggested that by reading the Bible, the Holy Spirit will enter you and give you this faith (Romans 10:17). Well, I read it cover to cover, as did countless non-believers and former believers before me, so that can't be it. Some suggest that you just need to place your trust in God and ignore your logic and reason if they contradict this trust, as explained in Proverbs 3:5, "Trust in the LORD with all your heart and lean not on your own understanding." The problem with this should be quite clear — this statement appears in the book that defines the LORD. This is no different than the self-validating statements that appear in dozens of other holy books. Ultimately, you are being asked to put your trust (faith) in a book, not God. And some suggest that you can only have this kind of faith if you *really* desire it. Now that makes more sense. But desiring to be certain something is true with no evidence, leads to deliberate and immediate dismissal of any and all contradictory information that is confirmed through logical proof and material evidence. Does anyone really want that?

Some say atheism is faith-based reasoning. Atheism is not a form of reasoning; it's simply the disbelief in God, just like not skiing is not a sport. Do atheists rely on faith in some of their arguments? If they believe in something that does not rest on logical proof or material evidence, then yes. Usually, however, beliefs are formed using some kind of evidence — even for the Christian. *Classical apologetics* is all about convincing others that Christianity is true by using material evidence. This is based on the idea that the non-believer requires such evidence to form their belief, then God or the Holy Spirit will take over and give them the faith they need for salvation. But what if the Holy Spirit, like Santa for the 16-year-old, never shows up? Or what about all those intellectual Christians who believe and practice Christianity based on evidence but lack the Biblical faith described earlier? I would sure hope that if the Christian God does exist, he would be loving and forgiving enough to save some spots in Heaven for these well-meaning individuals.

I would be lying if I didn't say that Biblical faith frightens me. Since the beginning of recorded history, there have been those who use this unquestionable faith in others to take advantage and manipulate them. Over a billion people count on religious leaders to interpret the Bible for them and tell them how God wants them to act, how God wants them to vote, and even how God wants them to think. Have faith, but have faith that your natural tendencies to question ideas and doubt "authority" are there for a reason. The Bible sums it up best: *"A simple man believes anything, but a prudent man gives thought to his steps."* (Proverbs 14:15)

Chapter 19: Atheists, What Proof of God Do You Require?

Very often in debates, the Christian will ask the atheist, "So what would you accept as proof of God's existence?" Almost always, the atheist gets all flustered and says something stupid like, "God to write in the clouds that he exists" or "A big booming voice coming from the sky saying 'I am!'" Really? That's the best you can do? I have seen much more convincing signs of the supernatural in a *Penn and Teller* magic show. An omnipotent God can certainly do better than that.

First of all, any reasonable atheist who is open-minded enough to accept the existence of God should not require proof, but rather accept his existence based on sufficient evidence. How do I *know* the earth is a sphere? From pictures, from what NASA tells us, from what I learned in school, etc. But I never went up in space to see it for myself. Even if I did, would that really count as proof or is it possible that some gravitational pull of light made it look that way? The point is, any lawyer worth his or her ridiculously outrageous hourly wage could easily argue against this kind of so-called proof. But, based on the evidence we do have, we can reasonably conclude with near certainty that the earth is a sphere. Atheists should be open to idea that they don't need proof, just sufficient evidence — more than the evidence that God does not exist.

A question we need to ask, before this question of proof can be answered, is what God are we talking about? A god who is responsible for the creation of the universe and that's it, or the traditional Christian God who is all knowing, all powerful, all good, and that constantly interferes with human affairs? Logically, the latter will require much more evidence.

What would I require as proof that the Christian God exists? Like I said, *I don't need proof—I just need more evidence that the he does exist than evidence that he does not exist.* However, if God were to give me or anyone proof of his existence, he can easily get into our minds and make us believe without question. But he cannot... I mean, would not, interfere with our "freewill". So I make the choice by my own freewill to allow God to bypass my freewill in this case and make me believe. He should have no problem doing this, since he didn't bother asking me if I wanted freewill before he gave it to me.

With today's technology, talented magicians and knowledge of psychological conditions, I don't believe the skeptic would accept any other form of "proof".

Chapter 20: Having an Open Mind

Every so often I come across a movie where the over-protective, cat-eye-glasses-wearing, martini-drinking mother will blame anything and everything undesirable on "the devil".

"Mom? Can I go to the school dance tonight?"

"Absolutely not! School dances are the work of the devil!"

In the movies I have seen, this scene is obvious satire. But sadly, it represents the mindset of a large percentage of Conservative Christian America.

To this very day, many practicing Christians believe that the devil (Satan, not the spokesman for the Dirt Devil® vacuum cleaner or the mascot for the New Jersey Devil's hockey team) is hard at work trying to take away the faith of the faithful by "leading them into temptation". This temptation, by many believers' standards, includes the quest for the knowledge and reason.

I can't help but see the brilliance in this design to attract and keep followers to the faith. According to many Biblical interpretations and religious customs, one is encouraged and expected to use reason in forming his or her belief. However, if you are presented with information that pulls you from your faith, it's "the work of the devil". But not all Christians hold to this belief. In fact, the head honchos in the Roman Catholic

Church actually embrace the idea of the faith-hating devil in helping to discover truth — as did God in the Bible.

The term *devil's advocate* actually comes from the Roman Catholic Church and it's clear that this traditional and revered organization supports healthy skepticism. From Wikipedia:

During the canonization process of the Roman Catholic Church, the Promoter of the Faith (Latin: promotor fidei), popularly known as the Devil's advocate (Latin: advocatus diaboli), is a canon lawyer appointed by Church authorities to argue against the canonization of the candidate. It is his or her job to take a skeptical view of the candidate's character, to look for holes in the evidence, to argue that any miracles attributed to the candidate were fraudulent, etc. The Devil's advocate opposes God's advocate (Latin: advocatus dei; also known as the Promoter of the Cause), whose task is to make the argument in favor of canonization.

If the Roman Catholic Church can use healthy skepticism to help discover truth, so can you. If your common sense, logic, and reason all are working against your beliefs, it might be time to reevaluate your beliefs.

Chapter 21: Just Wishful Thinking?

Theists have often been accused of embracing Christianity because of wishful thinking. It is great to think that there is a father figure always looking out for us. It is comforting to think of a world in which perfect justice prevails and all those who get away with bad things in this life will pay for them in the next. It is wonderful to think that when we die we are sent to this glorious place, in perfect bodies, where the streets are paved with gold and where we can eat as many Cinnabons™ as we like without getting fat. But what if there is no God? Then there would be no judge of our moral choices, no big-brother-like being watching our every move, and no ultimate accountability for our actions. To some, this is wishful thinking as well. Is everyone therefore guilty of wishful thinking?

Wishful thinking is defined as the formation of beliefs and the making of decisions according to what might be pleasing to imagine instead of by appealing to evidence, rationality, or reality. It is not possible to prove that someone else is guilty of wishful thinking since we cannot know how his or her decisions were formed. We can, however, get a good idea if we are guilty of wishful thinking by critically and honestly evaluating our beliefs. If you admit you might be guilty of wishful thinking, you will find yourself more open to critical evaluation of evidence, which will almost always bring you closer to the truth.

It is important not to confuse cause and effect here. For example, I believe my wife loves me and it's pleasing for me to imagine that my wife loves me. But this does not mean that my wife doesn't really love me. I am confident that my wife loves me by the evidence such as the way she holds me, how she takes care of me, and the fact that she tells me she loves me daily. I can honestly say that whether I wanted my wife to love me or not, I would still believe (without question) that she loves me based on the evidence alone. Can you say the same about your beliefs?

Wishful thinking is a form of emotion, and emotions often get in the way of our ability to make logical and rational decisions. Being in the "I don't really care if God exists or doesn't" camp myself, I find this a huge advantage in evaluating evidence for and against the existence of God and the truth of Christianity. There are some anti-theists out there who, for their own reasons, despise the idea of God or are militantly against religion in general. Their emotion leads them in the direction of wishful thinking rather than forming justified beliefs. When it comes to raw emotion and passion, just about every evangelistic, apologetic, and born-again Christian is swimming in it. This passion is wonderful for praising God and converting others to the faith, but lousy for rational and unbiased evaluation of evidence.

We are all guilty of some form of wishful thinking in our lives, but we don't have to be. We can be honest with ourselves and identify where we are letting our desires get in the way, and choose to evaluate evidence based on the evidence itself. It's not always easy, but it will, more often than not, bring us closer to the truth.

Chapter 22: One Billion Christians Are Wrong

The law of contradiction states that something cannot be true and false at the same time. This is one of the undisputed laws of logic adhered to by just about everyone, no matter what their religion. This law states that a duck cannot also *not* be a duck, a tree cannot also *not* be a tree, and the perpetual Virgin Mary cannot have any other children besides Jesus. Out of the roughly 2.1 billion Christians on this planet, about half of them consider themselves Catholic. Almost all Catholics hold the belief that Mary, mother of Jesus, remained a virgin for her entire life (thus perpetual). The other billion Christians disagree. So assuming that this belief is held by roughly half the Christians, a billion Christians out there are wrong, but which ones? And does it really matter? What can we learn from this?

Before we explore this any further, I need to define "wrong". If you are making a statement of opinion rather than a statement of fact, as long as you are being truthful, you cannot technically be "wrong". For example, "I believe Babe Ruth was the greatest baseball player ever!" is a statement of opinion, not a statement of fact. However, if your belief is contradictory to a fact, such as "I believe human noses have three nostrils," then for all practical purposes, you can be wrong. Since Mary either remained a virgin or she didn't, one of the two options must be right, and the other wrong. Assuming, of course, Mary even existed.

Countless papers and essays have been written by both sides defending their views on the perpetual virginity of Mary. It is not my goal to go through the arguments here, but for the sake of completeness, I will summarize.

In many verses in the New Testament, Jesus' "brothers" are mentioned. Catholics insist these are Jesus' cousins (or step brothers), since the Greek word for brothers is very broad and covers other family connections as well as "kindred spirits" as in "hey, wassup brotha!" The non-Catholic view maintains that the usage of this word makes it very clear that Jesus is referring to his blood brothers.

So who is right? We may never know for sure. More evidence may be uncovered in time, but you can be assured that this evidence will be highly disputed by the opposing side. Does it really matter? To Protestants, not really. To Catholics, the perpetual virginity of Mary is a very important component to their faith and tradition and, yes, it would matter a great deal if Mary did not remain a virgin.

This is where faith comes in. As a Catholic, you must have faith in the church and the conclusions they come to, despite what reason might tell you. As one who approached this matter with no theology to get in the way, both arguments being equally as strong, I have to rely on reason instead of faith. Either Joseph never knew his wife sexually the entire time they were married, or he did. Looking at the history of marriages, and being a man myself, chances seem pretty good to me that there was some "knowing" going on (if you know what I mean).

The fact that we now know that one billion Christians are wrong about this aspect of their faith leads us to the following questions:

Why are both views written with such conviction and authority if one of them has to be wrong? A spiritual leader, apologist, or representative of a religion must appear confident in his or her beliefs if others are to accept the belief, even if he or she is not confident. Christianity would not be where it is today if Jesus had said, "Uhhh.. I think you might want to love your neighbor... perhaps, if you want. Or I could be wrong."

How could the infallible Church make such a monumental mistake? The Catholic Church (or just "Church" with a capital "C") has earned my respect for apologizing for mistakes made in the past. However, they lost much of it by apologizing on behalf of the fallible people in the Church, not the Church itself. It is highly doubtful that no matter what evidence materializes, the Catholic Church will never admit fault — they can't.

How could what appears to be such an obvious fact in the Bible (according to Catholics) possibly be so wrong? The New Testament tells a partial story of Jesus. In fact, only the gospels really tell the "story" of Jesus (four stories, actually), the other books refer occasionally to Jesus and his sayings. Based on what we do know, we have to make reasonable assumptions to fully understand the life and teachings of Jesus. While it's true that the Bible never clearly says that Jesus had brothers and sisters from the same biological mother, it can be reasonably assumed.

How many other critical messages and meanings are getting "lost in translation"? Fundamentalists claim that any translation errors are minor and insignificant, yet call upon these "translation errors" to defend supposed contradictions that could prove the Bible errant. They can't have it both ways.

Do we really know as much as we think we know about the events that took place almost 2000 years ago? No, we don't.

What's the point of an inerrant Bible if it can only be interpreted by errant beings? I don't really have an answer for this one, it's just interesting to ponder.

What's the point of an infallible Church if every admitted mistake is blamed on fallible members of the Church? I don't really have an answer for this one either, just wanted to take a cheap shot at the Church indirectly by asking the question so I can still come across as the good guy asking a sincere question.

The perpetual virginity of Mary may seem like a minor issue, but Catholicism has many of these kinds of beliefs that stem from the single belief that Jesus gave the Apostle Peter the authority to run the Church as he sees best, and the authority to pass this power to anyone he chooses. Non-Catholic Christians disagree with this as well.

No matter how inerrant the Bible or infallible the Church may be, human interpretation and interference always has, and always will, get in the way.

Chapter 23: Spirituality: Not as Crazy as it Seems

Many years ago, out of pure intellectual curiosity, I attended a spoon-bending seminar at a "spirituality" retail store in Western Massachusetts. Spoon bending is the practice of bending spoons allegedly using supernatural forces. In a spoon-bending class or seminar, each participant brings in his or her own reasonably solid spoon to bend. When I came across the ad for this seminar, I thought to myself, "Now this I have to try!"

I walked through the store and headed toward the back room where this modern-day ritual would take place. On my way, I passed magical crystals, healing stones, manifestation jewelry, and even instruction manuals on how to communicate with the dead. Just as I was about turn around and run full speed for the door, a woman dressed like a carnival fortuneteller said to me, "You must be here for the spoon-bending seminar. Go right through this door." The fact that she knew that, really creeped me out — until I realized I was holding a spoon in my hand.

I was directed to one of the several chairs arranged in a circle all facing the center of the dimly-lit room. The smell of spicy incense filled the room as did the mystical sound of a medley of stringed instruments and angelic chanting (available on CD for just $9.95). While in my seat waiting to get started, a colorfully dressed woman next to me leaned over and asked me in a soft voice, "Do you believe in fairies?" At this point, I was ready to fake a heart attack in order to get out of there. But the seminar began and the woman who guided me into the room explained to us that we were to gently rub the neck of the spoon while envisioning a pyramid over our heads, which would channel energy from the spirit world, through our bodies, and into the spoon. Oh yeah, and we were told to keep trying to *forcefully* bend the spoon as well — but still letting the "supernatural energy" do most of the work. One by one over the next 20 minutes or so, the participants would shout in amazement as their spoon magically bent. I was the only one left with a spoon as straight as the path I had planned to take for the back door. Sensing my failure to harness the supernatural, the head spoon bender put her hands on my shoulders to channel her energy from her into me as the rest of the participants all cheered me on as if I were a frat boy getting ready to do a beer-bong. Out of pure desire to make this scene a distant memory, I bent the damn spoon. As I got back in my car to head home, I remembered thinking, "Is this what it means to be spiritual?"

Spirituality is a very subjective term. To most people, it's an existence outside our current physical reality. Some see this existence as the ultimate existence or the true reality. Some people believe that other beings dwell in this alternate realm of existence. Some believe that is where one finds ultimate happiness, *nirvana* (not the 90's grunge band), and even "oneness with God". The whole idea of spirituality appears to be quite "out there"... but it doesn't have to be.

To me, spirituality is not unlike our dreams, imaginations, and thoughts. The "spiritual world" exists because we exist — it's dependent upon our physical world; it's not apart from it. The only beings that exist in this spiritual world are the beings we put there. The idea of being *spiritual* is the ability to control our feelings and emotions from within while not allowing external conditions to get in the way. It is the ability to create joy, happiness, peace, love, and clarity completely from within. Most people never reach this *spiritual enlightenment* and spend their lives allowing their emotions to be manipulated by worldly events. This ultimately leads to a life of more pain and suffering than necessary. But the spiritually enlightened do exist. Some achieve this "enlightenment" through meditation, prayer, and/or contemplation combined with, or separate from, reading holy books including the Koran, Torah, Book of Mormon, New Testament, Analects, Veda, and others. Some discover their spirituality through crystals, astrology, or books by *Sylvia Brown*. As for me, I happened to simply realize that none of these methods, not even the fairies, are any more crazy than ignoring the fact that the ability to experience positive emotions, is all generated from within.

While I am far from a spiritual guru, I often am able experience what many people describe as a "religious experience," usually in a dream or dream-like state. The theists can say it's God that I am experiencing, the Buddhists can tell me it's nirvana, and Sylvia Brown can tell me it's the love of my dead uncle Billy. But seeing how this spiritual experience is shared by people all over world, from all different cultures, with very different beliefs, one has to look at the common denominator as the most likely source of this spirituality — the human mind. Although we might find the expression of one's spirituality "silly" or even "crazy", if it's bringing about real-world positive results, and it doesn't hurt anyone, what difference does it really make?

Chapter 24: How Would Your Life Be Different?

If you are a Christian, I ask you to imagine that you are an atheist. If you are an atheist, imagine that you are a Christian. How would your life be different than it is now? And more importantly, why would it be different? For the sake of this exercise, I will play on typical stereotypes of Christians being more "Jesus-like", since those who embrace Christianity strive to be more "Jesus-like".

As an atheist, if you did believe in God and in Christianity, would you start treating people better? Would you start practicing more forgiveness and showing more love to others? Would you stop doing the immoral things that you are now doing? Would you give more of your time and/or money to those in need? Would you change your career or just live life differently in any way? If the answer is yes, then why not live life this way now? You obviously feel what you would change is now "wrong". Do you really need the threat of Hell to live a good and moral life (according to your standards)? If you are living this kind of sub-standard life, perhaps this is evidence that the truth of Christianity is in the effect it has on lives, not in the stories it tells.

As a Christian, if you did not believe in God or in Christianity, would you start treating people worse than you do now? Would you show others less forgiveness and love? Would you start acting immorally? Would you stop giving to the needy and volunteering your time? Would you kick old ladies when they least expected it? If the answer is yes, you are no better than a criminal under the careful watch of a prison guard, and if I could, I would pay Big Tony two packs of smokes to beat the bjesus out of you in the courtyard. Why would you act differently? Are you really that much like a kid with no self-control, acting up when his or her parents are away for the weekend?

It has been suggested by theists that "if there is no God, all is permissible". What does that mean exactly? To be permissible, someone of authority has to be giving the permission. If there is no God, there is no one of authority giving permission. But let's assume that without God we have the authority and freedom to give permission to ourselves to do anything. Isn't this what freewill is supposed to be all about? The whole idea comes back to the idea of perfect justice. So the real objection is that without a perfectly just God there is no perfect justice. How can you argue with that?

I believe that Christianity gives people a reason to live the kind of lives they really want to live. It feels good to "do the right thing". It feels good to help others who are in need. It feels good to live life in a way that allows others to live a good life as well. But outside of Christianity, billions of people everyday find motivation and reasons for living a moral life. I would hope that Christians, despite a changing belief, would not turn to a life of anarchy. I would also hope that atheists would strive to live the best lives they can despite the lack of ultimate judgment. Take this mental exercise seriously and you might just learn something about yourself.

Chapter 25: You're In Good Company

Did you know that Sir Isaac Newton, Abraham Lincoln, and the Wright Brothers were Christians? Did you know that Thomas Edison, Thomas Paine, and Andrew Carnegie were atheists? Does it really matter? Can we say that we have Christianity to thank for human flight? If we do, we have to then give atheism credit for bottled light. For the most part, throwing out names of well-known historical figures or people currently in pop-culture headlines who share the same belief as you is a desperate attempt to show others that you are in good company with your beliefs. It is like saying, "I really don't know why I believe what I do, but this really smart person believes what I do, so by association, that makes me really smart — and right." But does the fact that some well-respected person shares the same belief as you, say anything about the belief itself? As a general rule of thumb, *it is not **who** has the belief that is important; it is **why** they have it*.

Christians have poster boy *Kirk Cameron*. I used to be a huge *Growing Pains* fan myself, admiring Cameron for his slick ability to talk his way through some challenging teenage situations. But Cameron did not become a child star because of his Christianity, nor did his childhood acting give him any extraordinary insight to the possibility of God's existence. Cameron is just a really charming guy who can probably convert a bunch of middle-age women who still have a childhood crush on "Mike Seaver". Christians also have Geneticist *Francis Collins,* head of the human genome project for over 15 years. Now here is a guy who knows more about what we are made of than perhaps anyone else on earth. Although he became a serious Christian at the age of 27 (33 years ago), the insight he gained from his research into the human genome did not cause him to lose his faith or change his belief.

Now let's look at who the atheists have on their team. On the one hand, they have *Kevin Bacon.* If you don't know who Kevin Bacon is, it's a mathematical certainty that someone you know does, or someone they know does, or someone they know does, or someone they know does, or someone they know does. But is Kevin world famous because of his atheism? No. He just apparently has a really good agent. Like Cameron, he possesses no superior insight to religion due to his acting. On the other hand, atheists have Physicist *Stephen Hawking,* a man who many believe to be more brilliant than Einstein. Hawking is said to know more about the cosmos than anyone — both in the past and present. When contemplating the mysteries of the universe Hawking doesn't buy the "God did it" hypothesis, because of what he does know. Hawking is an atheist because of his accomplishments and as a result of his accomplishments.

But even both Collins and Hawking have a very limited *professional* view on the existence of God in their respective fields. We have no idea what other factors contribute to their beliefs. Just because someone is famous for one thing, doesn't make them right about another thing — like actors who want to be politicians. Adopting the belief of someone you respect might appear to give you instant credibility, but it robs you of the journey of self-discovery, which leads to the confidence in knowing that your beliefs are not only true, but true to you.

PART IV: QUESTION EVERYTHING

Chapter 26: What Do You Really Know?

Socrates once said, "The only true wisdom is in knowing you know nothing." Or did he say that? Maybe he just wrote it. Or maybe he didn't say that or write it, but someone just attributed that to him. Maybe Socrates never even existed. How can we know? How can we know anything? This is the big question that has plagued philosophers for centuries. This is *epistemology*, or the theory of knowledge.

We know things by making assumptions. We assume that what we read in non-fiction books is true, we assume that what our teachers taught us is true, we assume our senses do not lie to us. We assume that the earth is not flat, we assume that we live in reality, we assume that other people exist outside of minds, and we assume that all the beliefs we hold as truth are true. But is anything really true regardless of our assumptions?

Some people reject the notion of absolute truth by suggesting all truth is relative. Some suggest that all truth is absolute. I would like to suggest, by making a logical assumption, that the "truth" is somewhere in the middle. Regardless of opinion or perspective, mathematical and logical truth exist. For example, 2+2=4 is objectively and absolutely true, for all practical purposes of the term "absolute". We can see this truth in our reality by taking two oranges, and adding them to two more oranges, and seeing that we have four oranges total. That fact that I am a handsome and sexy guy may be true to me, but unfortunately for me, many ladies may not see this "fact" as truth. In this case, we are simply confusing the words "truth" and "opinion". In fact, too many people use the word "truth" in too many situations when "belief" or "opinion" should really be used. In an earlier article, I already discussed the naturalistic foundation of truth, logic, and reason. But the idea of a supernatural existence of truth also exists.

If you believe that God is the foundation of all truth, realize what assumptions you are making. You are assuming your (priest, minister, rabbi, etc) is correct in his/her beliefs. You are assuming that God spoke the authors of the Bible and told them what to write. You are assuming that the authors wrote down exactly what God told them to. You are assuming that all the books in the Bible are inspired, and not added to the canon for any other reason. You are assuming that the dozens, perhaps hundreds of other supposedly divinely inspired books, with conflicting theologies, that did not make it into the Bible, weren't really inspired. You are assuming that all other early Christianities that were seen as heretical were, in fact, wrong. You are assuming that the group of people who established Orthodox Christianity over 300 years after Jesus' death was right. You assume it's God you communicate with, not Satan in disguise. You assume you are not delusional. But most of all, you assume that this truth is so eternal and unchanging that it's worthy of a capital "T".

No truth is established without a series of imperfect human assumptions.

Perhaps you believe we have some "sixth sense" that serves as a direct communication portal with God. Some describe this as intuition, "knowing in our hearts", or "knowing in our souls". If you do hold this belief, then you still need to realize that this does not bypass the fallible *human connection*. If your mouth speaks the words, "I talk with God," that message came from your brain, which you might believe came from your spirit, soul, or heart. At some point your human brain translated and interpreted this message. Anyone who claims to "know" anything through supernatural or divine agency, is still relying on their perfectly human brain's interpretation, which is often biased, flawed, and highly susceptible to influence.

I know only what I think I know, nothing more, nothing less. I take pride in the fact that I have no pride when it comes to having to be right. This does not mean that I do not accept truth and view everything with irritating skepticism; it simply means that I remain open to redefining what I hold as truth in light of convincing contradictory evidence and/or arguments.

As Confucius once said, "Real knowledge is to know the extent of one's ignorance." Or did he really actually say that?

Chapter 27: Anthropocentrism — Really?

In studying religion and reading the Bible, there is one reoccurring theme that is central to the teachings and it bothers me in so many ways: *Anthropocentrism*. This is a fancy word for the idea that humans are the center of universe. We are the purpose for all existence. We are separate from all other forms of life. We are God's ultimate creation. Everything exists for us. As my mom used to say, "What do you think, the world revolves around you?" No, mom, it now revolves around my kids.

Remember our silly ancestors who though that the earth was the geographical center of the universe? This idea was a reasonable conclusion based on what little information they had available to them. How about the Nazis who believed that the white race was the dominant race? Or our grandfathers who insisted that men were superior to women? These kinds of beliefs are ignorant and dangerous. Anthropocentrism is no different.

Once again we come to the idea of Biblical interpretation. While there are many parts of the Bible that give the impression that the reason there is something versus nothing is because of us, one can also use the Bible to show that God cares for his other creations (ignoring all the required animal sacrifices, of course). But no matter how many passages we can point to, the entire basis of Christianity, and theism for that matter, is the idea that God created everything for us. The reason that there are billions of other galaxies — us. The reason there are possibly billions of other life forms — us. It is all about us so we can "have a relationship" with God. Let's assume for a moment that God did create us to have a relationship with him. Why wouldn't he do the same for every other living organism? God would certainly be capable of this.

"But I'm special, dammit!" You sure are. You just need to change your idea of the word "special". You are not special at the *expense* of other beings; you are special *because of* other beings. Your being special does not mean other life forms have to be common or ordinary. You are different from the mosquito, the oak tree, and the biological pond scum. In fact, you are different from every other living organism on this planet. In this sense, you are special, but so is the mosquito, the oak tree, and the pond scum. It does appear that we are the most evolved species on the planet, a fact that makes us different from other organisms and perhaps gives us the confidence to assume our superiority in the universe. But this is a poor assumption considering the vast size of the known universe — and the human ego.

"But God created us in his image!" (Gen 1:27) Let's assume the "Bible says it, so it's true" stance. Even then, what the heck does this mean? We know God is pure spirit from John 4, so forget about the plump, grey-bearded God with eyeglasses of "The Far Side" comics. If we are like God in spirit, this means our physical brains have nothing to do with how we are like God. Separate from the physical body, spirits don't think, reason, see, hear, eat or poop. So why can't this same spirit of God's image be in every living organism? Perhaps God has revealed himself to every organism in a unique way that is independent of the physical form. We can't know this. So we assume we are "special" and it's all about us. Well, we are special, just like every other form of life on this planet, and perhaps on billions of other planets as well.

The universe has been here for 13.7 billion years and the earth for about 4.7 billion years. We have been here for only about 250,000 years. Think of it this way, if the universe were just 13 years old, we would have shown up 53 minutes ago. Like 98% of all species before us, we too will most likely disappear from the planet, and the universe, and its billions of galaxies will still be here. When admiring the sheer majesty of the universe, it appears that we are a byproduct of it, not the reason for it. We are a part of all life, and not separate from it. And I'm just fine with that.

Chapter 28: Heaven is "Up"?

*After he said this, he was taken **up** before their very eyes, **and a cloud** hid him from their sight. They were looking intently **up into the sky** as he was going, when suddenly two men dressed in white stood beside them. "Men of Galilee," they said, "why do you stand here **looking into the sky**? This same Jesus, who*

has been taken from you into heaven, will come back in the same
way you have seen him go into heaven." (Acts 1:9-11)

I would say that the position "up" is a representation that
allows us to associate this idea of Heaven with a place that has a
physical location. There are many people who take these
Biblical words literally and think Jesus floated up into the sky,
human body and all. But if this passage were meant to be taken
figuratively, why wouldn't the resurrection story as well? So
let's examine this.

The cosmologists tell us that up above the clouds there is
space, then other planets, then other solar systems, then other
galaxies, that extend for billions of light years. So Heaven must
be past the last galaxy — assuming there is a "last" galaxy,
which there really isn't. But even if there were, it would be kind
of far away.

In 2004, an international team of astronomers discovered a
galaxy **13 billion** light years away. So let's pretend Heaven is
right around there somewhere. Since the Apostles watched Jesus
rise up in the sky, he couldn't have been going that fast. Even
cruising up at 6 trillion miles per hour (speed of light), we're
looking at a total journey to Heaven of 13 billion years,
assuming, of course, we did discover the farthest galaxy from the
earth. If that's the case, Jesus is not at the right hand of God yet
— he still has 12,999,998,030 years or so to go. Did he have a
space suit? Did he have enough food and water for the journey to
sustain his human body? And was he even going in the right
direction?

We no longer live on a flat earth. That means that "up"
could be down depending on where you are in the world and
what time of year and day it is. So if it were the wrong time of
day, Jesus could have went "up" to Hell, and that would be a
total bummer. So only sometimes Heaven is "up" and other
times it's either below us or to the right or left of us.

These kind of ancient beliefs do actually make perfect sense
when they are put into a world with a flat earth and a three-story
universe (Heaven on top, earth in the middle, the underworld
below). It's just funny how today so many people still look "up"
to heaven to pray and tell their kids "Grammy and Grampy are
up in Heaven, watching over you". Assuming Grammy and

Grampy have amazing eyesight, it's possible that they are looking 13+ billion light years "up" at little Joey, not down.

Chapter 29: Heaven: It's Not What You Think It Is

Heaven is believed to be the most wonderful place imaginable where images of pearly gates, streets paved with gold, and little chubby angels playing harps fill our heads. Heaven is a place where good people go along with bad people who just happen to hold the right beliefs. It is place where all of your dead relatives are waiting for you with open arms. Heaven is a place of perfection. Or is it?

It will come as a shock to many, that the popular image of Heaven today has virtually *no* Biblical basis. Thanks to early Christian writings and art, such as Michelangelo's *Last Judgment* in the Sistine chapel, western civilization has adopted some imaginative views about Heaven which continue to been portrayed in books and movies to this day. In the days of the Old Testament, people believed in the three-story universe. We had the (flat) earth with its four corners where all of God's creatures dwelled, the "heavens" above, where God and the angels lived, then "Sheol" (mistranslated as "Hell" in the King James Version Bible) below where the dead "went" — in the Old Testament, this was *not* a place of punishment or torment. In the New Testament, Paul is quite clear that Jesus is raised from the dead, but *nobody else is*. Heaven is not a place where our "souls" are all reunited, but to the writers of the New Testament, Heaven will be *here on earth* and we will all be given new bodies while *living here* with God. So this means that currently Grandma and Grandpa are not watching you from anywhere — they're just plain dead (for now at least).

That's right. All this nonsense about spirits of ancestors floating in Heaven with God is either science fiction or comes from another religion (which is still science fiction). According to the Bible, Jesus' resurrection was the *start* of God's kingdom on earth. Early Christians, including Paul, were waiting "any day now" for Christ to return again and finish the job. 2,000 years later, 2 billion Christians are still waiting. Once Jesus and some "angels" exterminate 80% of all the people you know in the bloodiest, goriest, most violent, genocide ever imagined, this new "Heaven on Earth" will be all yours, according to the *Book of Revelation*. This is, of course, assuming you are among God's chosen ones. Here are some other questions to consider about Heaven:

Do you see your dead loved ones in heaven? What if your great aunt Edna loved you dearly but you really didn't like her at all. Are you stuck spending eternity with her?

Perfection is relative, is it not? What if little fat naked angels creep you out? What if you prefer the angels like the ones in *Victoria's Secret* commercials?

What bodies are you given? Are you given a new version of your old body before the maggots devoured it? Or your body as is? In the Bible, after Jesus was raised from the dead, he appeared to Thomas with his wounds and all. Sucks for all those people who died in tragic steamroller accidents. What about people born with birth defects? Or do all males look like Brad Pitt and all women like Angelina Jolie? Or do we even have a gender?

Do you retain your memories from your earthly life? Without a brain, how do you keep those memories? We know that memory is stored in our physical brains and brain damage and age cause us to lose memory.

Do animals go to Heaven? How about mentally challenged people who are unable to make moral choices? Or people with brain defects that cause them to act or think in a certain way. Where do they go?

If Heaven will actually be on earth, won't we run out of space? Some estimates say that over 100 billion people have lived and died so far. Even if 10 percent of those are saved, we will have some major overpopulation issues.

Where do all the people go who were alive before Jesus? Do they get a free pass or are they out of luck? In either case, is that justice?

How about those who never heard of Jesus? Is there some kind of "get to know Jesus" course before Heaven?

How about those who spend life worshiping the wrong God? There are billions of well-intentioned, spiritual, and deeply religious people breaking the first four commandments.

How about the lifetime murderers and rapists who accept Jesus on the electric chair? What will it be, perfect forgiveness or perfect justice?

Do babies and children age in Heaven? Or are they transformed into adults? Isn't our mental development dependent upon our experiences?

What if you have multiple spouses that have died? Do you become a heavenly swinger? How will your spouses feel about that? What if your spouse had multiple spouses they lost to death? How would you feel about that?

Now let's imagine this wonderful time has arrived. You are nothing like you are now. In fact, nobody you ever knew on earth is. You have a new body without the ability to feel sadness, sorrow, pain, remorse, frustration, anger and any other feeling or emotion seen as "bad". You no longer can make free choices since you cannot choose to do evil, wrong, or even make (and learn from) a mistake. God allows for evil and suffering here on earth so we can have the opportunity to help others, show forgiveness, compassion, kindness, and love. In Heaven, we no longer have that opportunity. Everything that makes us human will be stripped away from us when we are forced into a robotic-like existence worshiping God in a slave-like manner for all of eternity with no end in sight. You know, Hell might not be that bad after all.

Chapter 30: What the Hell?

Just like Heaven, our western culture's image of Hell has taken on a life of its own thanks to the imaginations of authors, poets, artists, religious leaders, and moviemakers. When we think of Hell, we think of a red devil with a pitchfork, blazing fires with screaming souls (I guess souls must have vocal chords and mouths as well), grotesque demons, and rap music. This is the place where bad people go — or good people who happen to have the wrong beliefs. Hell is perhaps the greatest, yet most manipulative, threat ever devised. But rest assured; it almost certainly does not exist.

It should come as no surprise that many other religions have their own version of "Hell" — many long before Christianity. It stems from our desire for justice. Death is not nearly a good enough punishment for the kind of lives some people live, so let's create a place where punishment continues in the afterlife. This doesn't make the idea of Hell false; in fact, one can argue that it actually gives more credibility to the idea. But we all know that people create religions, since they cannot all be true. This creation includes each aspect of the religion, and Hell is a major aspect that has been created by humans. For example, Hindu scriptures, which have been around long before Judaism and even longer before Christianity, describes

a dark world, filled with evildoers and their relentless cries of pain and agony, undergoing different kinds of torture and punishment as a consequence of their bad deeds in their previous lives.

But what about Judaism, which serves as the foundation of Christianity? Most modern translations of the Old Testament (the Hebrew Bible) do not even contain the word "Hell". If you are familiar with the King James Version of the Bible, you might recall that "Hell" is mentioned over a dozen times. This is a mistranslation of "the grave" that has been corrected in more recent translations. This "grave" (the Hebrew word "Sheol") is a physical location beneath the earth where physical bodies go when dead. But in Numbers 16:30+33, we see that the living can go there as well — kind of like visiting New Jersey. While this "grave" place is no Disneyland it's a place where the dead appear to "lie silent" (Psalm 31:17) rather than scream in eternal torture. Most importantly, there is absolutely no mention of people being sent to this "grave" because of what they do or don't believe.

In the New Testament, the idea of Hell becomes even more complicated. Hell is no longer a place for bodies, but a place for ghost-like images of the person. It is now a place of torment and anguish (Luke 16:23-24). This idea of Hell, usually referred to as "Gehenna" or "Hades", is a major theme in the New Testament as it's mentioned well over 100 times, about 70 times by Jesus himself. But Gehenna, often mis-translated as Hell, was really just a valley nearby Jerusalem that had a bad history. Yet Revelation does suggest a place of eternal torture. Confused yet?

So how did we get from the Old Testament underworld to our modern-day vision of Hell?

To me, the answer is quite clear. Early Christians expanded on the Old Testament idea of "Sheol" (the grave), adopted beliefs from other religions, added some stuff of their own, and cherry-picked select verses from the New Testament. They realized that avoidance of eternal suffering was a major motivator to get people to convert. Before the Gospels and the majority of the New Testament were written, Hell turned into a really nasty place. Remember it was many years after the death of Jesus that the first books of the New Testament appeared — more than enough time for the idea to evolve into a Christian belief.

I have read countless pathetic attempts from believers of Hell and the all-loving perfect God, trying to reconcile the two. What could any human possibly do to deserve an eternity of torment and suffering? Does rejecting Jesus as God really justify this kind of punishment? If there is a loving God, he is certainly not into sadistic torture, he is well aware that the humans he created are far from perfect, and he fully understands the biological and environmental factors, completely outside the individual's control, which influence one's actions, behaviors, and beliefs. If there is a loving God who is really desperate for people to believe in him and praise him, he would not resort to the threat of Hell to "encourage" people to believe. If God is love, or if there is no God, then Hell cannot exist. Either way, you can sleep well tonight.

Chapter 31: What Makes You, You?

I came across one of our home videos the other day of my daughter, Annabelle, and I playing together on a swing set when she was about two years old. I remember her little waddle, adorable giggle, and her tiny smile that was almost always hidden by her "binkie", which rarely left her mouth. "What happened to my baby?" I asked myself. Now, as an eleven-year-old girl, she is still adorable, but practically a different person. If she were in a different body, she would be unrecognizable from that two year-old in our home videos. So what makes up the "essence" of Annabelle or any of us for that matter? And can this essence survive after we die?

Let's look at a couple of the mind-blowing philosophical ideas on this topic, starting with the "You Duplicator". Imagine a machine existed that made an exact replica of you, down to the very last molecule. Would that other you be you? Would it have a sense of personal identity? How about the "Trillion Dollar Man"? (Sorry ladies, the female version is out of stock.) Imagine you were to get into a terrible accident, but the news is not all bad because this is much later in the future — a time when "they can repair you... they have the technology." The accident is really bad so piece by piece they start replacing your human parts with robotic parts. First your limbs, then your minor organs, then torso, then your heart, then everything else while saving your brain for last. Your brain is replaced with an advanced computer that works beautifully as your new brain, which retains all of the information held by your old brain. Are you still you? If not, at what point did you stop being you?

I think it's easier to determine what makes up the essence of a person by thinking of someone you know well and really care about. Imagine them in another body, completely different than their own (different race, sex, age). Of course, this is just superficial. But now imagine we surgically alter their brain and take away their memories. They have no recognition of you, of your history together, or even their own history. Now what if we remove the parts of their brain that causes emotion and feelings? Now what if we just kill the brain altogether, but keep the heart pumping artificially? Then we pull the plug. At what point do we say, "This is no longer my Uncle Waldo?" Or does it continue to be Uncle Waldo — just now he's dead? And where does the *soul* fit into all of this?

As we discussed in our chapter on Heaven, the cultural idea of the afterlife is based more on the works of science fiction and Plato, the ancient Greek philosopher, than the Bible. The idea of the soul being the essence of a person's being is a Platonic idea, as is the idea of souls meeting in Heaven with God. Ironically, this idea is not far off from early Gnostic Christian beliefs that were eradicated from the early Church and seen as heretical. Yet most people, not wanting to cease existing, imagine their soul, or *spirit*, being a ghost-like version of themselves. Many people who believe in the concept of a soul refuse to accept the idea that their memories, emotions, feelings, desires, and passions die with their physical body. If these human qualities do die with the physical body, even if the soul were to exist, when you die, "you" as you know yourself, are history. If this still is not clear, imagine what you were like before you were born — or at least when you were conceived.

We are constantly changing who we are both physically and mentally as every cell in our body is continuously dying and regenerating, as our brains process new information, as we learn from experiences, and as we change our morals and ethical beliefs. We rarely notice these subtle changes over time, but imagine the change with the instant loss of our biological self. If life does exist after death, will it even be "you" living it?

Don't let the idea of no longer existing get you down. You didn't mind for the billions of years of not existing before you were born, so why sweat the billions of years after? Live your life now.

Chapter 32: Where is Hitler Now?

I think most of us would agree that by today's moral standards, Adolf Hitler was a terrible man. I don't want to verbally recreate his atrocities, since I am quite sure that most people know what he did. But the question is: what happened to Hitler after he died? Assuming we die with our bodies, then his assumed suicide was his ultimate punishment and that's that. "Unfair!" you may cry. A simple and quick suicide is certainly not justice for a life responsible for the kind of human slaughter for which he was known. So there must be an afterlife where he pays for what he did. If there is, where is Hitler now?

Let's first look at this idea of fairness or justice. Many people cringe at the idea that Hitler got off easy without the eternal fires of Hell paying him back. Many people want this kind of justice so badly that for them, the thought of Hell not existing is... Hell. But desire alone does not lead to truth. Just because we want Hitler to be in Hell, doesn't make it so.

If there is a Hell, is Hitler definitely going there? We know Hitler had a very skewed idea of religion and God. Although a confirmed Catholic, his practices and actions went against Christianity in general. He might have used religion and God to win support and converts, and even attempt to justify some of his actions, but his beliefs remain questionable. But what if Hitler justified his actions by the actions of the God in the Old Testament? "Purging" the world of others, who were unlike you in some way, was not unheard of. In fact, that's pretty much the main theme of the Old Testament. As grotesque as it sounds, it's not hard to Biblically justify the actions of Hitler.

If you have never read the Old Testament, you may think that the idea that Hitler's actions can be Biblically justified is blasphemous or just outright wrong. Let's go with that. Let's now assume Hitler's actions were completely contrary to all that is good, which God desires from us. Were his actions against God's plan? For God to allow someone like Hitler to do what he did, there must have been a reason that we may or may never understand. So assuming that his actions led, or will lead, to a greater good, was Hitler just a tool used to make our world a better place? In which case, wouldn't he deserve a place in Heaven rather than Hell? But this doesn't seem right — according to what we generally perceive as "right". You'd have a better chance selling a Bible to an atheist than selling that idea to the descendants of the holocaust.

Let's try a different approach to see where Hitler is now. Let's assume Hitler gave up his Catholic beliefs later in his life. What if before killing himself, Hitler prayed to God for forgiveness, and accepted Jesus Christ into his heart as his savior? Does this assure him a seat next to God in Heaven? What about the decades of genocide and the millions of deaths for which he was responsible? You may wish for him to still suffer in Hell for a little, then maybe after some time (assuming time exists in Hell) move on up to Heaven, but this is mere wishful thinking and has no Biblical support. If he is "saved", he is saved.

What about forgiveness? Would Jesus forgive Hitler? Forgiveness and justice are often in direct conflict. It seems as if Jesus would do the forgiving but the God of the Old Testament would open up a serious can of whoop-ass on Hitler. But if Jesus and God are the same, what wins? Forgiveness or Justice? Maybe Jesus/God would forgive Hitler and allow him in Heaven, but when you get to Heaven, would you want to have a slushee with him at the local Heaven-Eleven?

Was everything Hitler did within his complete moral control? One can argue that anyone like Hitler must have had a few screws loose. To use a more technical term, it's very probable that his brain chemistry differed from that of a normal brain. How about his upbringing and his education? Did any of these experiences and physical characteristics play ANY role in who he eventually became? If so, how just is it to hold his soul morally responsible for the actions caused by his defective brain and life experiences over which he had no control?

So, where is Hitler now? He's probably six feet underground rotting away. I am not suggesting that there is no afterlife for Hitler — there is. Hitler will live on in the memory of billions of people who will forever know him as one of the cruelest people to have ever lived. Justice *is* being served and will continue to be served for as long as history never forgets the atrocities committed by one Adolf Hitler.

Chapter 33: Would You Slaughter Babies? Are You Sure?

Imagine you are out on a camping trip with your son. You hear a voice that you believe is God, telling you to take your son deep into the woods, and slaughter him (Gen 22:1-2). Would you do it? Or the LORD commands you slaughter every man, woman, and child in a neighboring town (EZ 9:5). Would you do it? Or what if the LORD commanded you to "utterly destroy" your enemies and "show no mercy" to them (DT 7:2)? Would you do it? What is extremely terrifying is that many God fearing Christians would answer an emphatic "Yes" to all three questions.

Many Christians form their image of God by reading select passages from the Bible, mostly the New Testament, which their church leaders suggest. When seeing God as we see Jesus, it's clear that we should strive to be like him. But what about the

God active in the Old Testament? Do we still see this God as the foundation of our moral values? It shocks me how many people devote their lives to the Christian faith BEFORE reading the Bible. Again, I am not talking about select passages that make you feel warm and fuzzy; I am talking about the entire book: the good, the bad, and the ugly — the very ugly.

But back to the question: What would you do if God commanded you to do something that completely contradicted your moral values, like butcher babies and little children (assuming slaughtering babies is against your moral values), simply because they were not from families who worshiped God? You might say that as a servant of God, you would do whatever he asked, having faith that he is asking you to do this for some ultimate good. Ironically, this is the same reason people give today when "God tells them" to drown their babies or murder their families.

Do our moral values really come from this God? When reading the Old Testament, I can't help but feel total sympathy for the countless victims of God's wrath — the Egyptian families who just happened to live in a country ruled by a jerk, every living being that didn't make it onto Noah's boat, and the 42 children mauled by bears at God's command (2 Kings 2:23-25). My moral values, wherever they come from, certainly cannot come from this God of the Bible, and I doubt yours do either.

If there is a such a line that separates good from evil, right from wrong, and justice from injustice, the God of the Old Testament has not only crossed it, but went to the opposite extreme on many occasions. I say this based on my subjective sense of what is right, moral, and just, which happens to be much closer to the views of our society than that of the Old Testament God. While it may seem "blasphemous" to criticize God, I have no problem with criticizing the ancient beliefs of the authors of the Old Testament.

If God commanded you to do something you felt was terrible, hopefully you would trust your moral values over what you think is God. After all, this "God" could really just be Satan.

Chapter 34: Prayer. Is There a Point?

People are very divided on the idea of prayer. Some see it as a direct communication with God and a means to ask for whatever they want, others see it as nothing more than talking to oneself. So where do these beliefs come from and more importantly, is there a point to prayer?

Prayer has been around long before Christianity when the recipient(s) of the prayers were many different gods and spirits. How else would one get it to rain if not by prayer or a ceremonial dance? Fast forward many years to the time of Jesus. Jesus was quite clear about prayer and the effectiveness of prayer:

So Jesus answered and said to them, "Assuredly, I say to you, if you have faith and do not doubt, you will not only do what was done to the fig tree, but also if you say to this mountain, 'Be removed and be cast into the sea,' it will be done. And whatever things you ask in prayer, believing, you will receive." Matthew 21:21-22

Jesus has reportedly said repeatedly (Mark 11:22-26, Matthew 7:7-11, Matthew 18:19-20, John 15:7, John 15:16, John 16:23-24) that **anything** you want will be achieved if you pray for it in his name. In some cases he throws in "if your faith is strong enough." Given these very clear and repeated assurances made by Jesus himself, it's quite clear why believing Christians put so much faith in prayer. But as we know, prayer, even by the most faithful, doesn't always work. Why not?

As a human I cannot help but get upset when my fellow humans are being taken advantage of. In the case of failed prayer, the reasons can be as benign such as "it's not God's will" or as emotionally devastating as "your faith isn't strong enough." The failure is no longer on the part of God, but on you, the pathetic human who is not worthy of having such prayers answered. Or even worse, in the case of evangelists and "healing" ceremonies, who say the limb you lost in the war didn't grow back because, "your financial offering was not large enough."

Intercessory Prayer

There have been several studies done on prayer over the years all with, as expected, "mixed results". This led to the *Templeton Foundation*, a well-known Christian organization supporting scientific discoveries, funding $2.4 million for a 10-year exhaustive study on what is called *intercessory prayer*, or praying on the behalf of others. The results were not quite what anyone expected. Those being prayed for, who knew they were being prayed for, did worse than the group not being prayed for. For a detailed description of the study and results Google *Templeton Foundation prayer study*.

Petionary Prayer

Petionary prayer is asking God for things you want for yourself. These can be very noble things like "courage" or very self-centered and materialistic things like "a job that pays more so I can get that new Mercedes." Usually, petionary prayer is something like praying to find a companion to share your life with, a cure for a terminal illness you might have, or less suffering from a temporary aliment. Does this kind of prayer work? This answer is not as black and white as one would expect.

If you pray to roll a one on a single die, your prayer will work about one in six times on average. However, if you pray for something that you have either direct or indirect control over, prayer can have a significant impact. Why the difference? We are only beginning to understand the power of our mind and its relationship to our physical body, but that connection is there and has been proven. This is most evident in the placebo effect. If you believe your mind or body will respond in a certain way, in some cases, it will be true. One can argue that this appearance of what nontheists call a form of "mind over matter" is nothing more than God doing his magic. But both the placebo effect and prayer — from one who believes in the effectiveness of prayer — have similar effects. This is independent of religion and faith.

The Philosophy of Prayer

We have already seen that Jesus talks about prayer in some detail in the Bible. It is also discussed in many of the letters from Paul and those written in the name of Paul, plus many times in the Old Testament. But does this idea of asking God for what we want conflict with our modern definition of God? Today, the God of the Bible is defined as an all-powerful, all-knowing, all-good, and personal God who is everywhere. If this accurately describes God, then:

If God knows what's best for us, why not just trust him with what he has planned for us? Who are we to question the will of God? If God wants us to have painful hemorrhoids, than so be it. One can even argue that running to CVS to purchase some "Preparation H" would be interfering with his plan. It seems like the whole idea of prayer is contradictory to having faith in a God who always does what is best for us.

If God is omniscient (all knowing), then doesn't he already know exactly what we want? It is believed that prayer is required because God can only "hear" us when we say something out loud or concentrate on thoughts so they can be "transmitted" to him. An all-powerful, all-knowing, perfect God would not have these kinds of limits. This God would know what you want, even before you knew. The act of prayer is not required.

What happens when millions of faithful, deserving Christians all pray to win the lottery? They can't all win. Does God pick favorites? How come atheists win the lottery too?

Some may argue that prayer is really just an act of faith to prove to God your devotion to him. Once again, an all-knowing God would not require proof of your devotion, furthermore a physical act by no means can represent the faith one has inside. Prayer is not for God; prayer is for people.

The Real Benefits of Prayer

Growing up, each night before bed my mom use to remind me to say my prayers. This included thanking God for all the good things in my life, and asking God to help those less fortunate. This is a wonderful practice that I believe has tremendous value. But as a non-believer, I cannot get myself to talk to a God who I don't believe is there, nor can I ask this of my children. But being consciously grateful for your good fortune does not require a god, and helping the less fortunate rather than asking God to, will be better for everyone.

Prayer is also directly related to hope. When all other options are exhausted, many people who would not consider themselves theists resort to prayer. I am reminded of George Bailey at the "end of his rope" praying for help AFTER he does the unthinkable — asks Potter for help. In a more personal example, several years ago, in my liberal Christianity days, I was suffering from cluster headaches — a kind of pain that can only be equated to childbirth (so they tell me). I did pray for the headaches to stop and sure enough they did — six weeks after they started — which is the typical cycle of cluster headaches. The hope of prayer is a great thing; something that the most certain atheist can call on if needed. Of course, prayer, when used in place of medical attention, especially on critically-ill children, is far from a benefit.

If prayer makes you feel good, gives you confidence, allows apparently miraculous changes to happen in your body then keep doing it. If, however, your unanswered prayers have led you to feel ignored or "abandoned by God" consider the possibility that prayer may be nothing more than the act of solidifying your thoughts and focusing on what you want. Sometimes you will get it, sometimes you won't. No God required.

Chapter 35: Prayer, Safety, and Planes

Your spouse is leaving on a plane to spend some time with a friend across the country. As a good Christian, and a loving spouse, you say a prayer for him or her after saying goodbye at the airport, asking God to see to it that he or she lands safely. Will this make a difference?

For the sake of this discussion, let's assume that the God does exist who can hear prayers and can interfere with our world. Let's also assume that God's overall plan for your spouse and the 200 other passengers on the plane really wasn't that important, and you actually are better qualified than God when it comes to determining the fate of others. Or we can assume that God's a bit flaky and really wasn't sure what he was going to let happen to the plane — he was considering allowing it to crash, but after your prayer he decided he would allow a bus full of underprivileged kids to go off a bridge instead, just to meet his disaster quota for the day. So let's assume that your prayer can have an effect on the outcome of the event.

How much will your prayer change the odds of the plane not crashing? 10%? 1%? .00001%? Now what if other people prayed as well for loved ones on the plane? By how much will that increase the probability that the plane lands safely? What if passengers pray? Are those prayers worth more or less? Are the prayers of Jews worth more or less than the prayers of Christians? What if a nun, a priest, and a rabbi are on the plane? That has to increase the odds of safely landing by at least 10%, no? If more babies are on the plane, does that increase the odds of safety? What if while on the way into the plane, a black cat ran in front of your spouse and he or she walked under a ladder while breaking a mirror that happened to be in the jetway? Statistically, the plane is much more likely to crash, is it not? But what if several of the passengers had their lucky rabbit's feet on them? I wonder if there is a mathematical formula for all this?

Luckily for your spouse and the other 200 passengers on plane, the plane lands safely at its destination. Not because of your prayer, the presence of the nun, priest, and rabbi, not even the lucky rabbit's feet, but because a safe landing with no fatalities is the most probable outcome (about 9 million to one). Yes, even though the plane was full of sinners including a hooker, an adulterer, and even an atheist.

Although quite ineffective in assuring safety, this kind of selfless prayer certainly will not hurt anyone in this situation. If it makes the one doing the praying feel better about him or herself for thinking of others, then great. If it reassures the one doing the praying and the one receiving the prayer by giving them hope, then that is wonderful. But most people spend a significant portion of their lives praying, yet they never really think through the whole concept of prayer. Prayer may be effective in some areas, but it certainly is *not* a superpower using God as a tool to violate the laws of nature and modify statistical probabilities. This kind of superstitious practice is an insult to our intelligence. But I will concede that at least with prayer, little bunny rabbits don't have to get their feet chopped off.

PART V: GOD

Chapter 36: You Need To Know the Whole Truth

Did you ever buy a used car only to find out later that there were numerous problems with the car that the salesperson conveniently left out in his sales pitch? Or maybe you hired someone who looked great on her resume, but later discovered that she neglected to mention her laziness, incompetence, and ignorance? Or what if you made a life commitment to a spouse who you thought you knew, only to find out later he or she has a dark side that would make the Unabomber look like Gandhi? If you're like most people, you would feel deceived, manipulated and taken advantage of. What the car salesperson, the employee, and the spouse did was purposely neglected to tell you the whole story, which would allow you to make an informed decision. Instead you are told a half-truth in order to get you to make a commitment, then, only after the commitment has been made, the full truth is revealed to you. At this stage, you are too far in to back out. You feel pressured into making excuses by telling your friends that your piece of crap car has given you a chance to learn about auto repair. You tell your boss that the lousy employee you hired just needs a little more training. You tell your family that your spouse, although gets drunk and smacks you around a few times a week, "really has a good heart." You continue to lie to yourself and live a life of conflict. You find yourself making more and more excuses as you are exposed to more of the truth. Have you been sold a half-truth about God?

Has anyone ever told you that God is forgiveness, kindness, and pure love? God may be these things, but he is certainly a lot more — at least according to the Bible. It has been said that the best "deconversion tool" the atheist has is the Bible. What Christians refer to as the Old Testament (the first 39 books of the Christian Bible) make movies like *Platoon* look like *Mary Poppins*. What is most disturbing about the stories in the Old Testament is not just the complete disregard for human life, not even the brutal methods of all the killings, but the fact that *God is the one killing*.

In the book, *Drunk with Blood*, the author calculated the killings of God in the Old Testament, either commanded by God or done by God directly, *to be almost 2,500,000 as reported in the Bible, but close to 25,000,000 that can be reasonably estimated* based on estimated population of the time. These are not all "sinning" men God eradicates; it's men, women, children, and babies. God doesn't just take away their life and let them fall to the ground peacefully, he drowns them (Gen 6:7), he burns them (Gen 19:24), he starves them to death (Gen 41:25), and those are the *kinder* methods. The fact that this Old Testament Biblical God is a "jealous" and very often "angry" God is in no way evidence that he doesn't exist; but it's evidence that this God might not be all about love and forgiveness. Perhaps it's true that all these men, women, and children did deserve the violent deaths they received. Perhaps God did have a reason for his "cruel and unusual" punishment methods. Perhaps he did do all this with love.

What about slavery in the Bible? We know that slavery was common in antiquity, and God appears to be a big supporter of slavery as made evident in many verses. But this doesn't mean you can do whatever you want with slaves. God makes it very clear in Exodus 21:20-21 that you can beat slaves all you want, just as long as the slave does not die within a couple of days of the beating. This is not a lesson learned in Sunday school — you need to crack open the Bible to find it. So how do you respond to this after you already accepted the perfectly loving and good LORD Jesus of the New Testament? You point out that for the day, this was better than how those without God treated slaves. Or perhaps "beat slaves" was mistranslated and really meant, "love slaves". As a "God of the Bible" believing Christian, you may even compromise your humanity in order to defend this God as portrayed in the stories of the Bible, like Fundamentalist Douglas Wilson did in a public debate with Christopher Hitchens when he agreed that beating slaves is morally good, because God "commanded it."

What about sexism in the New Testament as made evident by supporting the "sit down and shut up" role of women in Church? 1 Corinthians 11 is very clear that women are to be subordinate to men. I am not a woman, but if I were, I would question God's perfect justice. Remember, this is not just the writings of some misogynistic old guys from 2,000 years ago; this is, as believed by many, the "Word of God". I have read many Christian responses to this alleged sexism looking for a reasonable modern way to understand this — I have failed. It seems as though modern-day Christian understanding of this alleged sexism stems from C.S. Lewis' Book, *Mere Christianity*. The idea is if the man and woman cannot agree and they are in a "stalemate", then the man is right. Why? Because the man has a penis. Once again, the Bible believing Christian is forced to compromise on what he or she knows is wrong, in so many ways, in order to defend this inerrant Biblical idea of God.

It doesn't end with genocide, slavery, and sexism. The God of the Bible appears to condone xenophobia, homophobia, rape (look it up: Deuteronomy 22:28-29) and so much more that no moral person in the 21st century can possibly continue to defend. So how can the Jesus we all know and love as described in the *Veggie Tales* coexist with the God of wrath from the Old Testament? It can't, according to second century Christian philosopher Marcion. *Marcionites* believed that Jesus is so different from the God of the Old Testament that they must be two different Gods — the evil creator God of the Jewish Bible (OT) and Jesus, the kind and loving God who has come to save us from the evil God. This view was deemed heretical by the early church fathers and Marcion was excommunicated. Today, some believe that Jesus marks a "new beginning" between God and his people. Of course, this doesn't justify the "old" God's actions in the past. But most people are never introduced to the God of the Old Testament.

When it comes to religion, ignorance can be bliss.

If you want to know the truth, the whole truth, and nothing but the truth about the God of the Bible, do not limit your education about God to church services, Christian websites, and Christian Books. First and foremost, **read the Bible** — the whole Bible. Then, read books from both Christian and atheist authors. You might find yourself having to rethink some of your core beliefs, or you may find that knowing the whole truth reaffirms your core beliefs. But if you hide from the truth, afraid that you will lose your faith, then your kind of faith probably isn't worth saving.

Chapter 37: Presuppositions About God's Existence

Perhaps the most difficult aspect of examining the existence of God fairly, is the presupposition you bring with you to the process. First we define God, usually by Christian standards, and then decide whether we believe in this God or not. Depending on your belief, the "evidence" leads you to very different conclusions.

Take the resurrection of Jesus as an example. As a theist, you believe the Bible is the inspired Word of God, so that fact alone validates the resurrection story. Besides that, God is certainly capable of raising his own son from the dead — the guy created the universe so how difficult is restoring life to a single person? Any and all other possible explanations seem contrived.

As a nontheist examining the same evidence, you don't believe in God, therefore, not only can the Bible not be inspired by God, but the supernatural event of Jesus being raised from the dead is *extremely* improbable. ANY other explanation is more probable, including the idea that humanoids from the future traveled back in time and staged the event as a practical joke. Unbelievable? Certainly. But if you hold firm in your belief system that God not only doesn't, but *CAN'T* exist, than this time-traveling humanoid explanation is infinitely more possible.

With either belief held firmly — God must exist or God can't exist — you will not be capable of coming to unbiased conclusions. As a theist, you need to ask for God's forgiveness in advance and accept the fact that he might not exist (he will understand). If you determine he does exist after giving all evidence unbiased consideration, your faith will only be stronger. As an atheist, you need accept the fact that nobody can prove that God does NOT exist and understand that you are no less intelligent for opening your mind to his possible existence. If you determine he does not exist, you can be more confident that your belief is based on well-examined evidence rather than old presuppositions of questionable origin. If you are a Christian who was raised believing in God as a child, decided to accept Jesus as your savior as a way out of a life tragedy — or were convinced of his existence while smokin' some wacky weed with your collage philosophy professor — letting go of your previous beliefs and starting from scratch is probably a pretty good idea anyway.

Chapter 38: What Makes God, God?

In Chapter 31, we explored the idea of what makes you, you. As we replace 100% of your biological body parts with highly advanced robotics and super-computers capable of perfectly mimicking the human brain, then erase your memory, at some point most people would agree that you are no longer you. But what if you did not have a physical body, biological parts, and a brain in which to store a memory? What if you didn't even exist within space and time? If the question, "What makes you, you?" wasn't interesting enough, we will now explore the question, "What makes God, God?" Of course, we can just say that God makes God, God, and move on, but what fun would that be?

Let's start by a very basic introduction of the philosophical concept of *substance*, which is actually a pre-Aristotelian concept, although Aristotle usually gets the credit. Simply put, substance is the thing itself, apart from its properties and actions. For example, a pig is a pig not because it goes "oink," or has a curly pink tail, or it tastes delicious with eggs; it's a pig because of its "pigness". This is generally regarded as a metaphysical concept, so you cannot see a thing's substance under a microscope. According to the substance theory, God is God because of the substance of God. Wow, that's helpful.

Assuming you are not satisfied with the substance theory as a way to explain what makes God, God, we need to dig deeper and continue defining God. Since we cannot define God by describing his physical attributes, we are limited to his *properties* and *actions*. The properties generally associated with God are:

- God is omniscient (he knows everything)
- God is omnipresent (he is everywhere at once)
- God is omnipotent (he is all powerful — not to be confused with "impotent")
- God is pure love

- God is forgiving
- God is jealous
- God is kind
- God is pure good
- God is moral
- God is just
- God is a person (or 3 persons in one, depending on theology)
- God is a conscious being
- God is an intelligent being
- God is eternal
- God exists
- God thinks
- God is *non-temporal* (outside space and time)
- God is perfect in every way

The actions generally associated with God are as follows:

- God created everything
- God inspired the (Tanakh/New Testament/Qur'an)
- God did everything just as it is written in the (Tanakh/New Testament/Qur'an)
- God takes away life
- God gives life
- God chooses to save lives
- God answers prayers
- God judges people after death
- God chooses to give certain people the gift of grace
- God talks to people
- God listens to people
- God suspends the laws of nature to perform frequent miracles

- God unleashes his wrath upon us
- God loves us
- God desires our worship
- God impregnates human women
- God sees you when you're sleeping
- God knows when you're awake
- God knows when you've been bad or good...

These are the properties and actions that are generally associated with the Christian God, in the American culture, in the present day. Your idea of God may differ slightly from this representation of God — in fact, it almost certainly will. If you were to ask an Abrahamic-God-believing person every few hundred years, starting 3,500 years ago, to list the properties and actions of God, you would clearly see an evolving God. What's going on? Is an eternal God really evolving that much in a mere 3500 years? Or is our idea of God really a reflection of the people and the culture? Think George Burns in the 1977 movie, *"Oh God!"* versus the God in the book of Leviticus, and you will have your answer.

At what point does one go from a theist to an atheist? Obviously, if you accept all of the properties and actions of God in this list, you are a theist. If you do not accept any, you are an atheist. But what about everything in between? What if you accept that God created everything, but does not interfere with human life? What if you don't think God created everything, but do think there is a God father figure who watches over us? What if you think God had nothing to do with the Bible? Would this God of yours still be "the God?"

The more we define God, the more we create an impossible being. I am not suggesting that God is impossible; just that we put limitations on God by defining him with human concepts that are contradictory by definition. Can something that is all-powerful possibly exist? Can something that knows everything ever really think? Does it have to? Are perfect forgiveness and perfect justice compatible? Are forgiveness and wrath compatible? Can a "person" not have a physical existence? And we *know* that the many holy books that are believed by certain groups to be from God are not all compatible with each other. God is illogical. He is a round square, an invisible pink unicorn; a being, who can create a stone so heavy he can't lift it, an unstoppable force against an immovable object. He is his own father and his own son. He is 100% man, 100% God, and 100% really bad at math. God is a self-contained paradox. Many people have no problem with God's paradoxical nature because God is thought to exist outside of our natural universe; therefore God is not subject to natural laws. But this does pose a problem for the theist. God can't be illogical since our logic is supposed to be a reflection of the mind of God — a part of God. In fairness to God, he cannot be blamed for being illogical; it's humans who insist on giving him illogical qualities that make him illogical. By attempting to give God specific attributes, we are no different than our ancient ancestors who created myths to try to explain what they don't understand. Except that we should know better.

What makes God, God? We know it's not the way he looks, sounds, smells, feels, or tastes. We can say that he is God because of the substance of God, but in all practical terms, that is synonymous with saying God is complete nothingness. We can say that God is God because of his properties and actions, but then we run into a philosophical problem known as the *sorites paradox;* i.e., if we take away properties and actions one at a time, it's unclear at what point God is no longer God — it's just like taking away a single grain from a "heap" of grain, one at a time. **We make God, God.** Through a completely subjective process, we decide what definitions of God we find acceptable and which we don't. Some use sacred books as a foundation for defining God, some use what they call personal revelation or religious experience, and some use logic and reason. But even "revelation" and religious experience require interpretation using our imperfect and very human minds, which rely on logic and reason. Can this God, similar to the one described, exist outside of our minds and independent of us? We'll get back to that question later.

Chapter 39: Praise God!

I live quite a wonderful life for which I am very grateful. I have a loving wife, two amazing kids, and an excessively sweet dog. We are all healthy, happy, and well off financially. As someone who holds gratitude as a virtue, I want someone to thank for my good fortune in life. But whom can I thank if not God?

Some believe that God is fully in control of their lives and they just need to sit back and let God lead the way. I never believed in this. When I was a believer, I always felt that God would have given us the ability to control our own lives, so sitting back and waiting for God to do things for you would lead to nothing but disappointment. After all, it's more perfect for God not to have to be involved in our daily lives than to act as a father figure for billions of immature and irresponsible adults who refuse to take control of their own lives. Asking for courage and strength is one thing; but playing *World of Warcraft* all day while waiting for God to prompt Maury Greenberg, the VP of Personnel at Penatrude, Inc., to stumble upon your resume online and offer you the CEO position, is a different story.

Even though we appear to have control over much of our own lives, it would be ignorant of us to not acknowledge the many deterministic and influential factors in our lives. For me, I was fortunate to be born in a country, where knowledge and technology were readily available to help me survive a blood disease at childbirth. I was fortunate enough to be raised by upper-middle class parents who loved me and provided me with everything I needed to become a productive member of society. In fact, everyday I am fortunate for the continued health of my family. My blessings, as my mom used to call them, are quite common. But many people take them for granted.

So whom do we thank and praise for our good fortune outside of our control? Even if God were responsible for our good fortunes in life, God, in his ultimate perfection, does not lack anything and certainly does not need, want, or desire our praise. God is not a desperate parent buying his kids new cars and designer jeans hoping to buy their affection and love. The thanks and praise we give to God is for our benefit, not God's.

But if God does not need, want, or desire our praise, why is it so clear in that Bible that he does?

The God of the early Old Testament appears to have an inferiority complex by demanding worship to him and him alone. This is most likely due to the fact that there were many gods worshiped at the time. In addition, most Old Testament scholars acknowledge that in several parts of the Bible, it was evident that the writers of the Old Testament believed that other gods actually existed as well as "the God". Therefore, God is a "jealous" God (Exodus 20:5) and demanded worship to him, as opposed to the other gods at the time. He was so jealous, in fact, that the first four of the Ten Commandments are all about praising and worshiping him. At least this is according to ancient Jewish theology.

Forget what you think for a moment and imagine a perfect God who loves humanity. Imagine this God as the one who is responsible for your good fortune in life. Imagine this God as a perfect being who lacks nothing and has no needs, wants or desires. The best way you can glorify this God is by turning your gratitude into doing something for humanity rather than giving this God something he does not need, want, or desire. This may include working at a homeless shelter or soup kitchen, donating to a charity, helping a neighbor less fortunate than you, or doing anything to lessen the suffering or increase the happiness of your fellow brothers and sisters. I know this is much more work than just saying prayers or going to church on Sunday, but demonstrating your gratitude, rather than just talking about it, helps others as well as yourself.

If you believe in God, turning your gratitude into service for humanity is the ultimate form of praising and glorifying God. If you don't believe in God, turning your gratitude into service for humanity is a way to do your part in making the world a better place. Either way, both you and humanity win.

Chapter 40: Is it God We Need? Or the Idea of God?

It has been suggested that for every desire, want, and need, there is a corresponding object or action to fulfill that desire, want, or need, otherwise, we would not have them. I wake up in the morning and I have the urge to relieve myself. I then feel a rumbling in my stomach, which is the desire to eat. After, I want to do something to keep my mind and/or body busy. Fortunately for me, there are toilets to use, food to eat, and books like this for me to write. But what about this deep down desire that we all seem to share? This "longing" for something we can't explain? This feeling that something is missing in our lives? Is that the need for God in our lives? And if so, isn't that strong evidence that he exists?

Since the beginning of recorded history, in just about every culture in all four "corners of the earth" (to use a Biblical expression), man has embraced some form of a god or gods. In fact, before the enlightenment, the question wasn't *if* you believed in God, it was *in which* god or gods do you believe? There is a need, or desire, for something, but that something is not God, it's the *idea of God*.

In his 1943 paper, *The Theory of Human Motivation*, Abraham Maslow presented what he called our "hierarchy of needs". His theory states that we all have needs, wants, and desires and we pursue these in order, starting with our more basic needs. These needs are

Physiological – breathing, food, water, sex, sleep, homeostasis, excretion

Safety – security of: body, employment, resources, the family, health, property

Love/Belonging – friendship, family, intimacy

Esteem – self-esteem, confidence, achievement, respect of others, respect by others

Self-actualization – morality, creativity, spontaneity, problem solving, lack of prejudice, acceptance of facts

Unfortunately, many people struggle through life trying to meet even the most basic needs. When these needs are not met, there is and always will be this "longing" inside. This is what pushes us to meet our more basic needs so we can focus on the last one—self-actualization. In absence of being able fulfill these needs, we (both modern and ancient man) call upon God (or gods). It is quite amazing how many of these needs can be filled by the *idea* of God alone.

Ancient people prayed to the gods for **physiological** needs such as rain to water the crops and sun so the crops could grow. Today, people pray to God for **safety** needs; they pray for God to watch over them and protect them. They pray for good health and the health of others, and they believe in a God who promises eternal life, meeting one of our deepest desires: avoiding death. A God of pure love who is said to love everyone, regardless of whether they "deserve it" or not, certainly fills the **Love** need. People put full trust in God and he gives them the confidence that everything will be okay (**esteem**). Notice that just *believing* it will rain, you will be safe, you will live forever, you are loved, and everything will be okay, is all it takes to fill these needs.

Perhaps we, modern man, call upon God most to meet our **self-actualization** needs. God is the answer to all of life's questions to which we cannot yet provide answers. What is the meaning of life? How did life begin? How can we demine truth? Where does reason come from? What is consciousness? To whom should I pray to win the lottery? God, God, God, God, God, and *Lottorius* the patron saint of the lottery. We are problem-solving beings and it's hard for us to accept "I don't know" as an answer, so we create answers to satisfy this desire for understanding.

If you have not seen it by now, let me make this clear; it's not "God the being" that fulfills all these needs, it's "God the idea". This is strong evidence that *God the idea* exists, not God the being.

So what? If people are getting their needs met, does it really matter if God is just an idea or not? I would argue that yes, it does. Praying for rain is not as effective as creating an irrigation and water storage system. Praying for good heath is not as effective as staying away from cigarettes and McDonald's. Love of God is harmless as long as it does not come at the expense of neglected relationships with real people. Living life believing that you already know the meaning life robs you of the opportunity to discover this meaning for yourself, rather than being told by someone else what the meaning of your life is. Believing we already have all the answers is devastating to human progress.

I can honestly say that I am fortunate to live a very fulfilled life. I personally do not experience this longing that I once felt. This continual desire I do feel is a wonderful force that pushes me to my human potential and challenges me to keep learning, growing, and sharing what I know with others. This is the desire that not only makes life worth living, but makes life worth celebrating.

Chapter 41: God of the Past vs. God of the Present

When we were kids, my friends and I would all brag about a time in the past when we caught a fish "the size of a shark" or even caught "dozens" of fish in one day. When we were actually fishing together, however, we usually didn't catch anything, besides a few sticks. Of course, we were just kids who loved to embellish facts and use our imagination. It's funny how the God of the Bible is very much like that "fish the size of a shark" and in today's world, many people are just like my friends and me waiting around for a single bite from any size fish.

The God of the past was very active in the lives of ancient people, fought with them, talked with them, made stone tablets with commandments for them. This God of the past gave people magic powers that allowed them to part rivers, turn staffs into snake-eating snakes, and even command bears to maul children. This God would punish the wicked by giving them boils, turning their water to blood, and sending "angels" to slaughter entire villages. If God were on your side, you would live for hundreds of years with many worldly gifts and it would somehow just rain on your crops and not your neighbor's, since he was unworthy of such grace. The God of the past was big part of the physical world.

The God of the present is a very different story. So different in fact that he appears to be non-existent. He doesn't talk to us today from burning bushes; instead God is said to use inspiration to communicate with us through pretty sunsets. He doesn't fight our battles for us or send angels help us slaughter our enemy's children — we have to do our own slaughtering. He doesn't even carve commands in stone, he "writes them in our hearts". No longer do the wicked feel his wrath on earth; that is saved for Hell. No longer do the God-fearing people experience good fortune here on earth; that is saved for Heaven. God does not show earthly favor anymore to "his people". God-fearing individuals experience loss of family members, poor health, misfortunes, and even death at the same rate as everyone else. The God of the present is like a superhero with the ability to turn invisible, but only when nobody is looking.

So why would this God who once appeared to be so empirically verifiable literally disappear? It has been argued that with Jesus, everything changed and God's role in our world has changed as well. Some say God just needed to reveal himself to us that one time, and it has been done. Now it's up to us to accept him with faith. Or maybe it's possible that the God we read about in the Bible is just a series of stories created to illustrate how the authors of the Bible viewed God.

Perhaps one day I will see God in a crushed soda can and fall to my knees. Or I will pray to God for some extra cash, and find 6 months later that the IRS sent me a tax refund — then fall to my knees. Or maybe God will reveal himself to me as a bearded face in a piece of grilled cheese (grilled cheesus) — then I will fall to my knees. But I think I would prefer the burning-talking bush revelation where there's a lot less room for interpretive flexibility.

PART VI: THE BIBLE

Chapter 42: 10 Things You Need To Know About the Bible

When my 9-year-old son told me that he thought the Bible was a book about hotels, I realized he might not be the only one whose understanding of the Bible is not quite what it should be. I have Christian friends that have been reading *parts* of the Bible their whole lives, yet know very little about the book itself, its history, and its creation. Whether you are religious or not, here are ten things you really need to know about the Christian Holy Bible.

The Bible is the best-selling book of all time. Since the first printed publication in about 1450 CE, the Bible has sold approximately 6 *billion* copies. I really hope God is getting royalties. Because of this phenomenal sales record, the Bible defines our culture. So much of who we are and what we believe comes from the pages in the Bible. To better understand mankind, or at least Christian and Jewish cultures, you need to understand the Bible.

The Bible is a great book. I mean "great" specifically from a literary standpoint. Before I read the book, I thought it was just a bunch of religious doctrine, but it's so much more. It is a series of parables, myths, allegory, poems, songs, and history all intertwined with theology that has survived for thousands of years. There is action, adventure, romance, gore, horror, drama, suspense, fantasy, and even some porn (if you're into that sort of thing). The only thing it lacks, in my opinion, is humor. I found the Bible about as funny as a garbage bag full of abandoned puppies on the side of the road.

The Bible did not fall from the sky. In my six years of Sunday school, never was the origin of the Bible discussed. Any questions about its origin were answered with a firm and abrupt, "It came from God." If you believe in God, then I guess everything ultimately comes from God. I should have asked about the Bibles *earthly* origins. The Bible is really a collection of writings written by human beings over the course of 1,500 years. It was human beings who evaluated hundreds, perhaps thousands of writings over the centuries. Through long and sometimes violent "debates", eventually (some 340 years after the death of Jesus) settled on the 66 books that make up the (Protestant) Bible we use today. Although a very human process, Christian theology tells us that the Holy Spirit guided this process.

The Gospels (stories of Jesus) were written 35-65 years after Jesus' death. When one reads the gospels, it sounds as if omniscient authors were there, with Jesus, the entire time from his birth to his death. The fact is, there are no first-hand eyewitness accounts of the life of Jesus. While virtually all Biblical scholars agree to the approximate dates of the Gospels, the interpretation of the significance of these dates varies based on theology. I agree with the majority position held by historical Jesus scholars in that the Gospels are *theological interpretations* of Jesus' life and ministry, which over the course of the 65 years of oral tradition, have been altered and embellished. Evidence of this is clear when reading the Gospels in the order they were most likely written: Mark, Matthew, Luke, and John.

Many of the books of the New Testament are either anonymous or *pseudonymous*. Very few people realize that anonymous authors wrote the four canonical Gospels. Unlike other New Testament writings, the Gospels themselves do not claim to be written by anyone. The common misconception, especially before modern Biblical scholarship, was that "Mark", "Matthew", "Luke", and "John" wrote the gospels. However, these Gospels are not titled "Mark's Gospel" or "Luke's Gospel", but they are called "The Gospel *According to* Mark" and "The Gospel *According to* Luke". These titles did not even appear on the earliest of manuscripts (that have been discovered more recently) — they were most likely given the titles by some of the early church fathers hundreds of years after they were written. Why? If the Gospel is believed to be written by one of Jesus' own disciples, it has much more credibility. "Pseudonymous" means that the writing was not written by the person who claims to have written it. Thirteen of Paul's letters in the New Testament are claimed to be written by Paul. Seven are virtually undisputed, three are in question, and the vast majority of Biblical scholars agree that three of the letters were not written by Paul, but only in Paul's name. This was said to be done to give the message of the letter a little more "street cred". This is most evident because of the conflicting theologies and ideas in these pseudonymous letters that just don't match Paul's other letters. If you believe that the Holy Spirit guided the entire canonization process (picking all the books that would be part of the Bible), then it really shouldn't matter who the human author of any of these writings is. However, if you believed as the early church fathers did, that only early books written by those close to Jesus should be included — those with "orthodox" theologies of course — then there is a problem.

We don't have any of the original manuscripts. The earliest complete manuscript we do have is referred to as *Codex Vaticanus* and dated to about 350 CE. We do have several fragments dated as early as 125 CE, the earliest known as P52 (not to be confused with the 80's band the "B-52's"), which is a small fragment of the Gospel of John. This means roughly 200 years of manually copying and recopying occurred before the first complete manuscripts.

Prior to 1456 CE, the Bible was copied by hand. The Bible has been copied by hand, translated, retranslated, and modified over and over for 1300+ years. During this process, scribes would "fix" things that did not make sense and make notes in the margins that later scribes would work into the text. This opened the door for countless mistakes; even the opportunity to change things purposely due to the personal beliefs of the scribe. We know this for a fact due to the over 5,000 manuscripts we now have of the New Testament. What we don't know for sure: what exactly the scribal changes are and what the original text is. But again, if the Holy Spirit was guiding this process, then all the changes/copying errors made by the scribes are there by God's will.

Only about 10% of practicing Christians have ever read the entire Bible. I really do not like quoting statistics when I don't have a valid source — but this seems to be a well-accepted number on most Christian websites. If you believe that the Bible is the Word of God, what could possibly be more important than reading his book? What does this say about the true beliefs of these practicing Christians? Assuming this statistic is accurate, and most Christians believe the Bible to be the inspired Word of

God, then very few practicing Christians are getting the whole truth about God and the religion on which they are basing their entire lives (and afterlives!)

Archeology does not prove that the theology in the Bible is true. There is much misinformation in circulation about how archeology has "verified" the authenticity of the Bible. To many people this means that the theological claims in the Bible *must* be true since the remains of a town were found that was mentioned in one of the Bible stories. This is like saying that existence of the Empire State Building proves that King Kong was real. The Bible is not a history book, although there are many historical facts contained within the book. None of the wild theological claims in the Bible has ever been verified such as the discovery of Noah's Ark, the Ark of the Covenant, Jesus' empty tomb, or an MP3 of the talking donkey.

The Bible predicts and glorifies the end of the world (as we know it). The last book in the Bible, the book of Revelation, tells quite a violent story of Jesus' return to bring the Kingdom of God here on earth. To many Bible believers, this is Jesus' "Good News" (*Gospel*) even though it means the unimaginable torture, then slaughter of the majority of humans on the earth. Jesus himself believed that the end would come in his generation, as did the Apostle Paul. Fortunately for all of us, they were both wrong. Each and every generation since believed the world was coming to an end in their lifetimes. We know this through historical records of thousands of "end of the world" predictions since the time of Jesus. It is unfortunate that so many people fail to find peace and happiness in this life, and then passionately desire the end of it. No matter how loud the apocalyptic cries of some may be, I wouldn't suggest quitting your job anytime soon.

I encourage everyone to find out more about the Bible themselves by actually **reading it**. Sure, it may take about a year, but it will be worth it, especially if you are a practicing Christian already. Also, take the time to read some of the works of modern-day Biblical scholars and textual critics — both Christian and non-Christian. The Bible, as well as the story of the Bible, is a fascinating one.

Chapter 43: Bible Interpretation: Who's Right?

If there is one indisputable fact about the Bible, it is this: the Bible is widely open for interpretation. This is why according to the *World Christian Encyclopedia*, global Christianity had (in year 2000) 33,820 denominations. The WCE does consider a "denomination" an organized group within a specific country, but it's very probable that each denomination still holds some unique belief or interpretation that would differentiate them from other Christian churches. Let that sink in for a moment. The Holy Bible, the supposed "Word Of God", written/inspired by the God that "is not a God of confusion but of peace" (1 Cor 14:33), has led to all these different interpretations — some very much the same in core beliefs, but many radically different. How does one make sense of all of this?

If the Bible were understood to be ancient literature written by man, using parables and allegory, hyperbole and myth, imagination and poetry, then having so many interpretations is exactly what we would expect. However, the Bible is accepted by the vast majority of Christians to be the Word of God, or at least, inspired by God himself. It is difficult to imagine such a perfect God being such lousy communicator. A God who would allow for all original writings of "His Word" to be lost — and only copies of copies of copies (ad nauseum) to be discovered that have been translated, mistranslated, and hacked by scribes in attempt to insert their theological beliefs. It is difficult to imagine the "Holy Spirit" deceiving so many well-intended people who want to do nothing more than to serve God, by allowing for so many different, conflicting, and misleading interpretations of the Bible.

Consider the example of the historic Christian position of women in the church.

As in all the congregations of the saints, women should remain silent in the churches. They are not allowed to speak, but must be in submission, as the Law says. If they want to inquire about something, they should ask their own husbands at home; for it is disgraceful for a woman to speak in the church. (1 Cor. 14:33-35)

This seems pretty black and white. In many churches around the world this position is still held. However, in more "liberal" churches it was realized that it would be difficult to convert women (over 50% of the population) with such chauvinistic views. They write this off as "practice of the time" or others talk about a feminist revolt that had to be crushed. So is this still the Word of God or does this part not count, and if not, why not?

Or consider homosexuality. Most would agree that the Bible is very clear that homosexuality is an "abomination", yet there are many denominations that accept the homosexual and see no Biblical conflict. Take for example the *National Gay Pentecostal Alliance (NGPA)*, who conveniently translate the well-known Leviticus 20:13 verse that reads, *"If a man lies with a man as one lies with a woman, both of them have done what is detestable..."* to *"If two men engage in homosexual sex **while on a woman's bed**, both have committed an abomination..."* So in this case, God is obviously concerned with mattress ownership. For the record, I have absolutely nothing against the homosexual; my issue is with self-serving translations of the Bible over honest Biblical scholarship.

How could these differences possibly exist? To many, the answer is very clear: they are right and everyone else is wrong. Or they have the "Holy Spirit" and every single other denomination is being misled by Satan. You would think resolving these issues would be easy through God. There are literally millions (perhaps over a billion) people that claim to communicate with God. All they need to do is ask God the simple question, "God, in your infinite wisdom and kindness, please tell me which denomination and belief system is the most true to your Word." If God is used to giving advice on your love life, job search, what you should/should not eat or drink, etc., I would think this question would be reasonable for him to answer. But would this really solve anything? Since everyone would be given different answers, they would all claim that only they actually spoke to God, everyone else was misled by Satan.

Biblical interpretation is more of a revelation of your own inner beliefs than anything else. If you are gay, you will see where the Bible supports gay relationships. If you are a woman, you will see where the church empowers women. If you really don't want to keep to Jewish law, you will focus on how Paul stresses the Jewish law isn't important rather than focusing on what Jesus himself actually said about keeping the Jewish law. Perhaps this is what is meant when Jesus said, "seek and you shall find". Whatever the true purpose of the Bible, I am pretty sure it was not written so people can use scripture to confirm their own beliefs and/or forward their own political agenda.

History has shown that some bad people did some bad things using the Bible as justification. This does not make the Bible bad, just like throwing the Bible at someone doesn't classify it as a weapon.

The next time you hear something interpreted from the Bible by anyone, realize that it's just one interpretation. If your denomination does not encourage you to question the taught interpretations, then find another denomination that does. If God gave you your own mind, it would be an insult to him not to use it.

Chapter 44: Do Biblical Contradictions Exist?

Most Christians either believe that the Bible is the literal Word of God or at least that the Bible was inspired by God. Given this, the Bible, as believed by many, cannot contain any errors (inerrant), even though the creation, duplication, and interpretation of the Bible is a very human process that occurred over thousands of years. But what if the Bible did contain factual errors or contradictions? Some believe that this would prove that the Bible couldn't be the perfect Word of God. The concern is, if you cannot believe *all* of the Bible, how can you believe *any* of it?

For the sake of this discussion, a contradiction can be defined as *a statement or a proposition that contradicts or denies another or itself, and is logically incongruous.* So for example, "Kim is married to me, but I am not married to Kim" is a contradiction, because it cannot logically be true. But what if I were to say that statement was meant to be more *allegorical* in nature, and what I really meant was that I am not fully committed to my marriage? Then it would make perfect sense, and no longer be a contradiction. Technically, the statement itself is still a contradiction; it's the interpretation and/or implied meaning that suggests otherwise. I am very committed to my relationship with my lovely wife, Kim (legal disclaimer).

What appear to be contradictions can also be explained in many other ways as well. Here is how most of the alleged Biblical contradictions have been explained:

Combination. Something can be more than one thing at one time. For example, my kids are both Irish and Swedish.

Time is ignored. A person can be both a child and an adult — at different times in his or her life.

Translation issues. Words can be translated in many different ways, especially from dead languages used 3,500 years ago. Biblical literalists suggest that if the accepted translation causes a contradiction, then there must be another way to translate it.

Vague language. "Brother" can mean biological brother, step-brother, or homie (yo, wassup brother?). If you are Catholic, Jesus had homies. Otherwise, he had biological brothers.

God is a logical contradiction. Since God is not bound by logic and is outside the laws of the universe, anything goes. God can be all things at one time, he can be everywhere and nowhere, he can be seen and not heard or heard and not seen, neither or both. You can't put worldly limits on God, therefore the Bible can get away with quite a bit.

Subjective words. Is God's anger is fierce and endures long (Num 32:13 / Num 25:4 / Jer 17:4) or is God's anger slow and endures but for a moment (Ps 103:8 / Ps 30:5)? It depends on how you define "moment". Or as Bill Clinton put it, "It depends on how you define 'is'."

Not the full story. It is very easy to pull a few words from the Bible and completely change the intended meaning. If you do not know the Bible that well, you can easily be manipulated by quotes taken out of context.

Specific for an audience. Jesus tells a man in Matthew 19 that he needs to "sell everything" in order to have treasures in Heaven. It would be a real bummer if we all needed to do this for salvation, so it's not a requirement for everyone, just to random men that Jesus tests.

Science is just plain wrong. So far we have seen explanations for the Bible contradicting itself and even the Bible contradicting logic. But what if the Bible contradicts generally accepted scientific theories? If the Bible cannot be wrong, then science must be wrong. Saddles on dinosaurs — deal with it.

As we know, the Bible did not fall from Heaven. It is a book that comprises 66 other books. Do you think that whoever established the canon we have today would have chosen books with blatant contradictions with the other books? Don't you think that this just might have been an important factor in the canonization decision process? I tend to agree that many of these apparent contradictions are due to the lack of understanding of the original and intended meaning — at least how it was understood at the time these books were accepted as part of the Holy Bible.

It is important to keep in mind that many of these alleged contradictions weren't a problem for ancient Judaism or early Christianity. Many of these "problems" are due to the evolution of theology over the last 2,000 years and our ideas about God that have become more cultural than Biblical. This is where the Bible certainly does appear to be problematic. For example, the idea that Jesus is God, or the doctrine of the Trinity.

I am tempted to list more examples that I see as real problems — more problematic for classical Christian theology than the Bible itself, but I am sure they can easily be justified by anyone determined to defend his or her faith. If you were to research Bible contradictions, you would find many sources listing several hundred. Ignore these sources. Instead, search for "Bible contradictions explained" or "Bible contradictions answered" and read the explanations and justifications given. Use your own mind to see if they make sense; not because you want them to, but because they actually do.

Those who insist on an error-free Bible are concerned that if one cannot believe the entire Bible, then one cannot believe in any of it. If I shared their views, I would be much more concerned with the practice of explaining away contradictions and different theologies through implied allegory, translation issues, vague and subjective use of language, and other linguistic acrobatics. Such an unclear, subjective, and non-literal book hardly seems like the work of a perfect God.

A contradiction is only a true contradiction if it cannot be explained, and the given explanation is accepted as valid. This is why some believe the Bible has over 600 contradictions and others believe it has none. If you honestly evaluate these apparent contradictions and conclude that some are actual contradictions because the explanations seem clearly contrived, you don't need to abandon your faith; but you do need to reconsider in what or whom you should be placing your faith.

Chapter 45: What About All the Fulfilled Biblical Prophecies?

Just days after the terrorist attack on the Twin Towers, I received a e-mail from my aunt who forwarded it from her BFF, who forwarded it from her husband, who forwarded it from his boss, who forwarded it from her cousin's piano instructor, who forwarded it from some guy named Dan, and so on. The e-mail contained a short message, followed by what appeared to be an excerpt from two of Nostradamus' quatrains...

This is incredible! Nostradamus predicted this event almost 500 years ago! Forward this e-mail to EVERYONE you know!

In the year of the new century and nine months,
From the sky will come a great King of Terror...
The sky will burn at forty-five degrees.
Fire approaches the great new city...
In the city of york there will be a great collapse,
2 twin brothers torn apart by chaos
while the fortress falls the great leader will succumb
third big war will begin when the big city is burning

A six-second Google search revealed that his e-mail was a complete fraud — a major hack of Nostradamus' actual quatrains.

Why did so many people believe this? I know my aunt had no intention of deceiving me, but we all love a good mystery mixed with a little magic. This is why books about Nostradamus, books by Edgar Cayce, and TV shows like the *Psychic Friends Network* do so well.

And what about all the prophecies in the Bible? How can one explain what appears to be the fulfillment of perhaps thousands of Biblical prophecies?

Once again we dive into the nebulous area of Biblical interpretation where we see two extremes, and everything in between. On the one hand, conservative Christian literalists maintain that the Bible contains no failed prophecies, just ones yet to be fulfilled. They also assert that hundreds of prophecies have already been fulfilled with amazing accuracy that can only be explained by divine intervention. On the other hand, non-believing Biblical scholars insist that no real prophecies have been fulfilled. Furthermore, hundreds of prophecies have failed with no chance of future fulfillment. How can people on both sides possibly justify these extreme opposite views? The answer? **Biblical interpretation.**

Without a doubt, one can certainly spend a lifetime researching the prophecies in the Bible. However, nobody should be expected to verify each and every claim to determine if Biblical prophecy does have some truth, nor should they blindly accept these claims simply because they want them to be true. This is an area where I would suggest you to spend some time to research the topic for yourself. Be sure to research both *Biblical Prophecies* as well as *Failed Biblical Prophecies*. But before you do, consider the following:

How specific is the prediction? Horoscopes, fortune cookies, palm readers, and all other believed indicators of the future use very general language that can apply to many situations.

Must the interpretation resort to symbolic or figurative language? The great thing about being a prophet is that you can never be wrong if those who interpret your prophecies resort to symbolism or assume figurative language.

Is this a desperate attempt to fulfill a known prophecy? I still can't get over the story in Luke where Jesus "borrows" a Donkey and rides into town. Could it be that the author of this Gospel threw that in just to make Jesus fulfill the Old Testament prophecy in Zechariah 9:9 where the king rides into town on a donkey? Yes. Frequently in the New Testament the authors go out of their way to say things like, "But this has all taken place that the writings of the prophets might be fulfilled". In other words, the characters in the stories are basically acting out a script.

Could the writing be much later than suggested? Biblical scholars have overwhelmingly agreed since the end of the 19th century that Daniel was written 400+ years after most conservative Christians believe. In fact, *postdiction*, or writing a "prophecy" *after* it has happened, is believed to be a common occurrence in many sacred documents.

Are there any sources outside the Bible that confirm these historical events that supposedly had taken place? In the book series *Harry Potter*, a prophecy is written that is fulfilled in the last book. Despite that fact, most people (not all) do not think these events really happened. Without multiple sources, we cannot be certain of anything.

For thousands of years people have been rushing to scripture to try to make sense out of a current situation. Without a doubt, the same verses have been used over and over again for centuries as a prophecy of a current event. This is called a *presentist* interpretation of the Bible. A great example of this is the BP oil spill. Some presentists suggest that the verses from Revelation 8:8–11 predicted this environmental disaster:

"The second angel blew his trumpet, and something like a great mountain, burning with fire, was thrown into the sea. A third of the sea became blood, a third of the living creatures in the sea died, and a third of the ships were destroyed ... A third of the waters became wormwood, and many died from the water, because it was made bitter."

With over 31,000 verses, the probability of NOT finding a verse in the Bible that can be made to fit virtually any modern-day situation is next to zero. But what if you had 2,000 years of history to play with? It's not difficult to see how quickly these "fulfilled prophecies" can add up.

It has been suggested by many Christians that Jesus was the fulfillment of several hundred prophecies in the Old Testament. However, Jews see things very differently. Jews maintain the Hebrew Bible is not proof for anything in the New Testament regarding a Messiah and have "refuted" each and every prophecy that Jesus supposedly fulfilled. Of course, if they believed that

Jesus were the Messiah, they wouldn't be Jews. Jewish comedian, Lewis Black, talks about how the Christians read the Jewish Bible and constantly misinterpret things. He sums it up by saying, "It's not their fault; it's just not their book." No matter who is right, it's clear that we are working with some *very* flexible verses.

The argument for Biblical prophecy, while it appears on the surface to be a strong argument that the Bible was inspired by God, is rarely used in any serious religious debate. Perhaps the primary reason is that the Bible itself warns of false prophets who can predict future events. Even if all the prophecies in the Bible were true, who is to say they are from God? Many people today believe in supernatural prophecy unrelated to God, and many Christians fear these prophets as being "from the devil". But the bigger problem is validating these prophecies using acceptable standards of Biblical scholars, textual critics, and historians.

The real question is, were the prophecies in the Bible written by prophets divinely inspired by the God of the Bible? Believing this to be true is not a question of fact, but one of faith.

PART VII: CHRISTIANITY

Chapter 46: The Growth of Christianity

It is estimated that approximately 2.1 billion people, or about 33% of the world's population, consider themselves Christians today. In the United States alone, there are about 225 million Christians or 85% of the population. In addition, many studies conclude that Christianity is on the rise, especially in countries such as Africa and China. So how did Christianity get to be the largest religion in the world today and why does it keep growing even in this age of enlightenment? Doesn't this fact alone prove the validity of Christianity's claims? If Christianity is not true, does this mean that around 85% of all Americans are delusional?

Let's start at the beginning — over 2,000 years ago in the Middle East where Christianity was born. At the time, there were the Jews, who worshiped the one God of Israel, and there were the *Gentiles* (non-Jews), most of whom were *pagans* or *polytheists*. Along came Jesus and his ministry. A handful of Jews followed Jesus in his three-year ministry up until the time of his death. Shortly after the crucifixion of Jesus, Paul the Apostle, who many regard as the "co-founder" of Christianity, started to spread the religion *about* Jesus, which soon became known as Christianity. This effort by Paul, many believe, is the reason we have Christianity today.

For the next 280 years, Christianity would continue to spread at a reasonable rate. Rodney Stark (sociologist of religious history) writes in his book, *The Rise of Christianity*, that this growth rate of about 40% growth per decade is about the same as the growth of the Mormon Church in the 20th century. So it was not that miraculous. But why did it even catch on? Christian tradition holds that the disciples and many of the apostles of Jesus were able to perform miracles. If this were true, it would certainly be a great conversion technique. But the moderate and study growth of early Christianity can be best explained by more historically verifiable possibilities. Here are just a few:

It was a religion that encouraged conversion. Unlike other religions, Christianity emphasizes the importance of converting others. You convert people whom you care about in order for them to be "saved" as well. Kind of like an early form of multi-level marketing, but instead of selling $30 all-natural toothpaste, the product is salvation.

It provided possible solutions to real problems. Need more rain? Ask God. Need more sun? Ask God. Need that nasty rash to go away? Stay away from the town prostitute, then ask God.

It told stories of miracles. "My God is bigger than your God" was a common conversion argument. Christians told stories of Jesus' miracles and how he created the universe and everything in it. Pagans had a hard time matching that with their pathetic gods who only seemed to be good for little things — like helping with digestion.

It was a much-preferred alternative to the strict Jewish law. "You want to cut what?" I would imagine was a common complaint of the time. Paul made it clear that circumcision and about 600 other really specific Jewish laws weren't necessary under Christianity.

The promise of Heaven is wonderful. Life is short but eternity isn't. Sign up today and receive eternity with God in paradise. If you act now, we'll throw in some Cinnabons in the afterlife.

The threat of Hell was terrifying. But if you don't call within the next 30 seconds, you will burn forever in Hell.

People believed they were in the "end times". For thousands of years, every generation had those guys on the street with the cardboard signs warning people about the end of the world. For thousands of years, normal people like you and me believed them. Christianity prepares people for this "good news" (well, good for most Christians at least).

Things really picked up in the year 312 CE, when emperor Constantine, the leader of the Roman Empire, converted to Christianity. This was a huge win for the faith, which led to many more conversions. Sixty-eight years later, in 380 CE, the Roman Empire officially adopted Christianity as its state religion. Fast-forward around 1,630 years and here we are with over 2 billion Christians.

Christianity continues to spread for many of the same reasons as it did two millennia ago. Conversion is still a major focus of the faith, Christianity promises to provide solutions to all of life's problems (if your faith is strong enough), miracles are still said to occur (although a lot less impressive as old school resurrections and strolls on water), Heaven is still a place just like Disneyland (but much less expensive) and many people still believe the end of the world as we know it's coming any day now. But in more modern times we can add a few more reasons to the mix:

People are born into Christianity. The odds are overwhelming that a person born into a religion will remain in that religion. As more Christians breed (and Catholics certainly do), they create more Christians, even if "Christian" just on paper.

The Church has become a major influence, source of power, and persuasion. No need to get conspiratorial here, it's quite well understood that the Catholic Church specifically has tremendous influence over a billion people, many of whom are registered voters.

It helps in politics. Quick, name a Jewish U.S. President? How about a Buddhist? Muslim? (No, Obama doesn't count) If you want to get far in politics, or just be accepted by the majority of people, you need to believe what the masses believe — or at least pretend to. That may change in the future, but for now we are still intolerant when it comes to religion.

It has become a social practice. I know of many non-believers who go to church just to socialize with others and take part in community events. And I am quite sure many women attend church just to show off their new shoes.

The Bible is like a big fortune cookie. The Bible is a huge book that contains thousands of stories, parables, sayings, and one-liners that can mean virtually anything you want them to mean. Like fortune cookies, the power is in the person who interprets and believes the message, not the message itself. But as these passages are interpreted to provide solutions for modern-day, specific problems, more and more people believe in the supernatural nature of the Bible.

Christianity offers up the love of Jesus. Unconditional love is one of the most wonderful experiences for humans. Unfortunately, many people do not have anyone with whom to share this kind of love. Enter Jesus. Despite what many people believe, it's the act of loving that gives people warm and fuzzy feelings, not being loved. As long as the lovers of Jesus do not demand signs of love in return, one can be happy in this (apparent) one-sided relationship.

The threat of Hell is terrifying. Wait... did I already say that?

It is the logical fallacy known as the *appeal to popularity* to assume Christianity is true based on its impressive 2,000 year run and massive following. Just because all the "cool" kids are drinking wine coolers at the eighth-grade dance, doesn't it make it okay. Christianity is still the minority belief in this world with over two thirds of the global population identified as "unbelievers" (of Christianity).

Ideas spread for many reasons other than their truth. Think of genocide, Communism, Eugenics (selective breeding in humans), racial segregation, slavery, and every other really bad idea that gained acceptance for many other reasons than truth. Wide acceptance of an idea does not give validity to the idea; it just gives it wide acceptance. An idea that is widely accepted does, however, give the idea credibility when it comes to others' *perceptions* of the idea. While it's hard to imagine that 85% of Americans are "delusional", it's not hard to imagine that 85% of Americans could be forming a reasonable belief based on an already commonly-held belief.

The growth of Christianity over the centuries has been without a doubt, very impressive. Its continual growth today is an indicator that people all over the world are still finding convincing reasons to believe. Christianity may be true, or it may not be. Either way, it's not going away any time soon and if we don't believe its theology, we should at least understand it.

Chapter 47: Born to Be Bad?

One of the central concepts of Christianity never sat well with me. This is the concept of *Federal Headship*. This is the term used in Christianity to explain Adam's (the first man, therefore our "father") relationship to us. It is said that because Adam sinned, that we (yes, even you) are responsible for and guilty of sin. In other words, you are born a sinner. This part really does not bother me because I do not believe in "sin" or the literal story of Adam and Eve and the talking serpent. But what does bother me is that many Christian brothers and sisters in life accept this idea of Federal Headship as part of God's "perfect morality".

Before we continue with the concept of Federal Headship, I want to make it clear that God is God and can do whatever he likes. If he wishes to torture babies while sending a thunderous laugh throughout the world for all the parents to hear, so be it. He is God. This does not mean that we have to like it. Most Christians HAVE TO believe that anything God did in the past, does now, or chooses to do in the future is not only acceptable, but it's pure good and morally perfect. This is what bothers me. So what is God doing under Federal Headship? He is holding children of every generation responsible for the sin of one man.

It is not unreasonable for a father to be held responsible for his 5 year old who ate a candy bar off the shelf while shopping at Wal-Mart. The father should pay (in this case financially) for the harm done to Wal-Mart (65 cents). Now if the father snagged the candy bar, it would be silly, and unjust, to make the 5 year old pay for it. But what if it weren't the father of the 5 year old that took the candy bar; what if it were the great, great, great, great, great grandfather and we still demand payment from the kid? Now what if we did not just demand simple payment for this crime, but held the child morally responsible for the crime of his great ancestor? I don't think there is a person alive that would see this as the morally right and just thing to do. However, this is exactly what the idea of Christian Federal Headship is about, and because God does it — as a "good Christian" who believes this Federal Headship — you must see this as morally right and perfect justice.

Christian apologist Matt Slick, explains, and attempts to justify, this idea of Federal Headship on his site carm.org by asserting that without Federal Headship in place, Jesus could not be our savior — because he would otherwise have died for nothing. To me, this is like urinating on your kitchen floor and when your significant other screams, "Why did you do that?" saying, "Because if I didn't, you wouldn't be able to clean it up."

The Bible can be interpreted to justify virtually any point or action. The Bible seems to indicate that for the most part, sons are not held accountable for the sins of their fathers and even when it does hint that God's wrath is poured onto the children of the sinners, it's only for 3 or 4 generations. There are passages that make it look like we are all sinners and others that make it appear that children are free from sin. However, nowhere does the Bible say anything like, "We all inherited sin from Adam." So is it a Biblical fact that we inherited the sins of Adam, or is this just one of the many interpretations of scripture that got passed down generation to generation without anyone stopping and asking the basic question, "Does this seem morally wrong and unjust to anyone? Is this something that a perfectly moral and just God would do?"

Who am I to question God's judgment or morals? Compared to God, nobody. But I am a representative of the human race and I seriously question actions like these to serve as the basis for morality and justice. And if Federal Headship is perfectly moral and just, then the words "moral" and "justice" are meaningless.

Chapter 48: It's All or Nothing, Baby.

I had always taken the position that any form of liberal Christianity made more sense than the fundamentalist, evangelical, Biblical literalist position held by relatively few Christians (percentage wise). I have many Christian friends who believe in the Christian God as well as the resurrection of Jesus, but certainly don't take many of the more "mythical" stories in the Bible literally such as Noah's Ark, the talking donkey, Tower of Babel, Jonah and the fish, and many others. But the more I studied the Bible, I began to realize that these more liberal forms of the faith require serious interpretative flexibility, and in some cases, start to unravel the core of Christianity.

What about the story of Adam and Eve? Is this a mythical tale with some theological overtone, or is it a historical fact? If one were to take this as historical fact, this story — not unlike the many Greek myths about the gods — would certainly go against countless mainstream scientific facts and what we today accept to be common knowledge. But if one did *not* insist this were a historical fact, we find some major problems surrounding the death and resurrection of Jesus.

If you've never cracked open the Bible to this story, take the time to do it. The story of Adam and Eve is a wonderfully written tale about how God created the first humans on earth completely free of evil, sin, and even death. Then along comes a serpent and encourages Eve to eat from the forbidden fruit tree. Eve, being the stereotypical, trouble-making, scapegoat of a woman she is, shows a little cleavage and gets Adam to take a bite (of the fruit). From this point on, all of humankind is cursed with sin. Most religions do their best to make it quite clear that we are born dirty, filthy, and unholy creatures in desperate need of salvation. How's that for a little self-esteem booster? But after a couple of thousand years, God sends his son/himself to earth in human form as a human sacrifice to himself to erase this original or *ancestral sin*. But if the story of Adam and Eve is a fable, what did Jesus actually die for?

If you believe in the accuracy of the New Testament, Adam must have been a historical figure just as stated in the book of Genesis. It is unquestionably clear that the authors of the New Testament, as well as Jesus himself, considered at least the first five books of the Bible as scripture — or the "Word of God". In Luke 3:23-38, the author traces Jesus' genealogy back to Adam. Paul refers to Adam in 1 Corinthians 15:45, *"Thus it is written, 'The first man Adam became a living being'; the last Adam became a life-giving spirit."* And there are several other places in the New Testament where Adam is mentioned. But more than that, the idea of sin and death being brought into this world through Adam is mentioned in Romans 5:15, *"Therefore, just as sin came into the world through one man, and death through sin, and so death spread to all men because all sinned".* These are clear references to the literal creation story, not some generic "first man" to eventually evolve into a human from a more primitive life form. And here's the kicker, if Adam did not exist, then he didn't bring sin into this world, then Jesus' death had no theological point, then the foundation of traditional Christianity collapses.

So what can we reasonably conclude from this? Either the creation story in Genesis is a historical fact, or the New Testament does contain factual errors. If the latter, the Bible certainly cannot be the inspired work of a perfect God, in which case, we MUST look at the Bible from a historical perspective rather than insist that it must be true simply because it's the inspired Word of God. I'd have to choose the latter. When we do read the Bible from this perspective, things really do make a whole lot more sense.

Chapter 49: What's Wrong with Traditional Christianity?

So many people confuse the benefits and harms of religion with the existence of God. In debate, you will hear both theists and atheists attempting to prove or disprove the existence of God based on arguments surrounding religion's, or Christianity's, overall effect on societies. This kind of argument tells us much more about the person's desire for God to exist or not exist, rather than the possibility of God's actual existence. But the fact is, Christianity, like virtually all established religions, has its benefits as well as its dark side. In this chapter, we will take a look at this dark side.

To be more specific, let's focus on the question, "How does traditional Christianity harm our society?" While I am certain any anti-Christian can produce a long list of alleged problems with Christianity, when you start to dissect these problems they can almost universally be reduced to the same single, but quite serious problem: *the assumed divine authority of the Bible.* Here is just a short list of societal problems generally associated with Christianity.

- Killings in the name of God

- Promotes intolerance through the belief that it contains the only absolute truth

- The spread of scientific and historical misinformation

- Misuse of the Bible by fringe groups to justify horrible actions

- Accepting laws given to a culture 3,000 years ago as today's moral and ethical standard
- Promotes sexism and homophobia
- More focus on securing your place in a possible afterlife than focusing on doing all you can in this life
- Teaches children that they are born sinners in desperate need of salvation which leads to low self-esteem
- Excuse to act immorally and not take responsibility for one's own life: "God's not done with me yet" or "I'm a sinner!"
- Failure to cherish other forms of life

As you can see, without the insistence that the Bible is the Word of God, none of these would be issues. What if the US Constitution was believed to be sacred and unchangeable? What was written and adopted back in 1787 made sense for the American people back in 1787, but the founding fathers were well aware that as society evolved, so would the need for the governing laws. Since the writing of that document, 27 amendments have been ratified which gave us freedom of religion, the right to a fair trial, protection from cruel and unusual punishment, and the abolishment of slavery, just to name a few. To this very day the "Word of God" holds firm that we should have no other gods before him, which is understandable... it's his book. But "trials", as suggested in the Bible, are far from fair according today's standards, God never took back his commands for stoning people to death, and he certainly never told us that slavery is wrong and we should free all slaves.

The Bible is believed to be the unchangeable Word of God. The only reason this book is still used today by reasonable, civil, and good people is because they have found ways to reinterpret the Bible to match today's cultural norms. However, none of these reinterpretations are universally accepted in the Christian community and the Bible is never "amended". This leads to all of the problems mentioned above and many more. But as we will see, despite these problems, Christianity has given humanity much for which to be grateful.

Chapter 50: What's Right with Traditional Christianity?

As one who doesn't accept the supernatural, it's easy for me to dismiss Christianity as an ancient belief system that has long outlived it usefulness. In fact, this was my position for most of my life. But this changed when I devoted the time to learn more about Christianity from a variety of sources, rather than sticking with sources that agreed with my position. One can say, "I was blind but now I see!" (John 9:25). As my understanding of Christianity grew, it became clear to me that this faith played a crucial role in our history and it continues today to shape our world.

Perhaps the most well known historical events in early Christianity are, unfortunately for Christianity, events that Christians would rather forget. The Crusades, the corruption in the Church, the witch hunts. But given its 2,000-year history, they're doing a pretty good job. As an American, I would rather forget how we "negotiated" our land from the Native Americans, how we fought with our brothers in the Civil war, and how we ended World War II — and that was only a few hundred years of history. History is full of events we'd rather forget, but we choose to remember them in order to create a better future. Christianity provided an alternative to the 613 extremely strict Jewish laws as well as the many pagan religions of the time, some of which included rituals harmful to children's health — like child sacrifice. Sure, Christianity wielded the threat of Hell like a 10 year-old wields his new BB gun, but it was still an improvement over existing religions of the time. Are we better off today because of Christianity? I think so.

What's right with traditional Christianity today, or to be more specific, how does traditional Christianity benefit our modern-day society? It gives people a road map on how to live a good life. It may be hard for a non-Christian to see this benefit, especially one who is perfectly capable of constructing his or her own road map. But everyone isn't like you and me. There are many people who, without guidance, are "lost". There are many parents who should not be responsible for the moral guidance of children, but thanks to Christianity, these children have a better alternative. Churches and youth groups provide second homes to many people who desperately need them. Church leaders are like the parents that many people never had and always wanted. Christianity helps people, who need it, realize they can have a second chance at life.

Perhaps the greatest contribution Christianity has made, not just to the societies that embrace Christianity, but to all the world, is the concept of charity. While the idea of charity existed long before Christianity, it was Christianity (credit attributed to Jesus) that focused on and promoted the idea as a way to show love to your neighbor (and God). You might still have a problem with giving credit to Christianity for a concept that has been around for centuries prior, but think of Jesus as the Bill Gates of the concept of charity. Gates was responsible for bringing the PC to the masses, just as Jesus was the man responsible for bringing the concept of charity to the masses. Without Christianity, charity would most likely not be as widespread as it is today and without Bill Gates, I would probably be typing this book on a typewriter. Furthermore, according to the *Social Capital Community Benchmark Survey* in 2000, religious people (people who attend church at least once a week — including Jews) are 25 percent more likely to give than secularists. This seems to be in line with similar surveys conducted by different organizations. I wouldn't conclude that religious people are more generous; just that they are encouraged more often to give and reminded more often of the people who need their help.

If you haven't figured it out by now, every single benefit I discussed of modern Christianity **is not dependent on insisting that the Bible is the authoritative Word of God**. This is assuming that church leaders provide support for their congregation out of the pure desire to help people and not out of the fear of God, and Christians give their money and time because they want to show love to their neighbors, not because they want to avoid Hell or attempt to "buy" their way into Heaven. Call me a sucker for the good nature of humanity, but I do believe that's the case.

Christianity does offer benefits to society. This, we should not overlook.

PART VIII: JESUS

Chapter 51: The Jesi

Everyone knows Jesus. He is that really nice guy with long hair, beard, compassionate eyes, and a great pair of sandals (aka "Jesus Jumpers"). But how do we know this Jesus? And how accurate is our *idea of Jesus* versus the real Jesus, if there even was one?

There are three primary existences of Jesus, which I will call "the Jesi" (pronounced Jeeze-eye). One existence we can be sure of, the other two we never can.

The Historical Jesus. When we study the historical Jesus, we try our best to determine who Jesus really was and what he really said based on the **original** sources we have, and the reliability of those sources. However, these sources can only give us a picture of what Jesus *probably* said, *probably* did, and who he *probably* was, because this is only what we can determine from recorded history — and that is assuming we accept the books in the New Testament as historical documents. Even autobiographies of people alive today can only take a "snapshot" of who that person really was. This is not the real Jesus.

The Theological Jesus. This is the picture of the Jesus we get from reading the Bible and accepting what we read as truth, or, the Jesus that is revealed to us in church. This also includes the Jesus with whom Christians claim to have a personal relationship. This is the Jesus that is "in the heart". Like the historical Jesus, the theological Jesus is derived from the very little information we have on Jesus, but unlike the historical Jesus, excludes sources deemed "heretical" like the gospel of Thomas and other Gnostic sources. This is not the real Jesus.

The Real Jesus. This IS the real Jesus. This is the Jesus that will forever remain a mystery. This is the Jesus that would fill in the gaps created by our knowledge of the historical Jesus and verifies or disproves the theological ideas of Jesus. You may be thinking, "I know the real Jesus; Jesus is love." Cheers to that. However, by "real" I am referring to the Jesus of flesh and blood that was born, walked the earth for 30 something years, and died — assuming he ever lived. What was allegedly recorded of Jesus' life was a tiny fraction of everything he did and said, everywhere he went, everyone he met, etc. Until Doc Brown perfects the flux capacitor, the real Jesus, we will never know.

It is important to realize that everyone creates their own Jesus in their mind as a result of what they are taught, what they read, what they see, what they imagine, and most importantly what they believe. Just like snowflakes, no two Jesi are the same. Realizing this will allow us all to be more understanding and tolerant to differences in the Christian faith.

Chapter 52: Who Was Jesus if Not God?

Christian apologist and Irish-born British novelist, C.S. Lewis, popularized the *Trilemma argument* back in the mid 20th century. This argument was meant for all the people who reject Jesus as God, but insist that he was still, "a really cool dude with great morals and a kick-ass teacher," or something to that effect. The argument was simple: if Jesus was not the LORD, he was either a liar or a lunatic. So all of those who are trying to kiss up to Jesus (just in case) while still appearing to be a rational thinker, still have a little more thinking to do about Jesus.

Let's expand on this argument for a moment. Orthodox Christians believe that Jesus made it quite clear that he said he was God. This would mean that if he were not God, he is lying, or he is mentally ill. You need to choose one of those options. Here is another choice for you. Your favorite ice cream is raspberry pecan shell, orange toothpaste, or butter bug crunch. Choose.

It should be clear by now that these are both good examples of *false dilemmas* — where you are presented only select choices when there are more to consider. What other options are there if Jesus was not God? Here are just a few:

- Jesus really didn't say all that was attributed to him in the Bible

- Those sayings where Jesus claimed to be God are not clear and can have other meanings, plus, there are many sayings attributed to Jesus that make it clear he is not God.

- Jesus believed he was "one with God", just as millions of people today believe they are "one with God"

- The story of Jesus we read in the Bible is more of legend than historical fact

- Jesus was dyslexic and he really just wanted people to call him "DOG," as in, "Wassup Dog?"

All five of these options are perfectly valid and probable with historical and/or scriptural evidence available to back them up — with the exception of perhaps that last one. (1) Historical Jesus scholars will tell you that if Jesus existed (which he probably did), *some* of his sayings and deeds are more likely to be authentic than others. Although this is still technically speculation, it's based on careful evaluation of other early Christian writings, comparisons of early and later manuscripts, and probabilities based on the theological implications of the sayings and/or deeds in question. (2) Jesus never said, "I am God," he said things like "I am" not much unlike Descartes, "I think, therefore I am." Jesus also made it pretty clear he was not God in Mark 13:32 when he said, "No one knows about that day or hour, not even the angels in heaven, nor the Son, but only the Father." (3) In John 10:30 Jesus said, "I and the father are one." Is it more likely he is referring to a logical impossibility, or that he was using his usual style of figurative language to express what he believed was his spiritual connection with God? (4) Suggesting that the Jesus story is more legend than historical fact requires a detailed explanation. This is covered in the next three chapters. (5) Some of the lesser-known symptoms of dyslexia include turning water into wine, healing the sick, and walking on water (don't bother looking that up — it's not really true).

So who was Jesus if not God? Anyone you want him to be. Jesus has many sayings and deeds attributed to him that are open for wide interpretation. This allows the reader of the Bible to make Jesus into the person he or she wants Jesus to be, rather than accept Jesus for who he really was and will most likely forever remain — a 2,000-year-old mystery.

Chapter 53: Was Jesus Superman or Batman?

There is an ongoing debate as to who is the better superhero, Superman or Batman? Superman is a being from another world who possesses super-human powers. Superman grew up as a human, but despite his humanness, will always be a Kryptonian. Batman is a human who possesses no super-human powers, but uses what human powers he has to maximize his human potential. In addition, he uses his resources to create gadgets that help him become more "super". While we can all be in awe of Superman, I can't help but have more admiration for Batman as a man who makes of the most of what he has, without relying on super-human powers. For this reason, he is an inspiration as the potential of human achievement. The orthodox belief is that Jesus was Superman. But I think he was Batman, which makes him even more worthy of admiration in my book.

There is an entire field of study within Christian theology called *Christology*, which deals with this nature and person of Jesus Christ. In other words, *Christology* calls into question his divine status. This is an area of study for which very few Christians are familiar, since most Christian leaders do not want to even acknowledge that Jesus might have just been a man. The canonical scriptures tell several stories of Jesus that can all be interpreted very differently when it comes to the divinity of Jesus. Many groups in early Christianity such as the *Adoptionists* and the *Ebionites*, supported the view that Jesus was fully human only. It wasn't until hundreds of years after Jesus' death that the views held by orthodox Christians became "orthodox". What if Jesus were just a man?

Imagine a radical Jewish preacher who comes with a very different message; a message of peace and love in a time when "stoning thy neighbor" was common practice. This preacher was a confident, well-spoken man with a message so powerful that people were sold on his message, by the message alone. This preacher did not need help from God to convince people that his message was worthy of following. The power was in the message itself, and the messenger had the charisma, courage, and fortitude to see that this message reached as many people as possible. Now imagine how great this man must have been, knowing that he was just a man.

As time passes, fact turns to fiction, stories turn to legend, and Jesus, a man OF God becomes Jesus, the man God. No longer are his works of human origin, but they are works of God. No longer do people believe that a simple man could have possibly delivered such a powerful message, but he must have had divine help. No longer was Jesus the Batman who represented the pinnacle of human achievement, but he became Superman, the humanoid that none of us can ever be.

Chapter 54: Why Do Jews Reject Jesus?

The first question that came to my mind when diving into the fascinating world of Christianity was, "Why do Jews reject Jesus as the savior?" Jews were, after all, there in the time of Jesus, and Jesus was a Jew! Do Jews know something Christians don't know, or is it the other way around? There are a myriad reasons why atheists reject Jesus, but why would one of the most traditional religious groups reject Jesus as the Messiah? For this question to be adequately answered, one cannot simply read arguments from Christians — unless that individual wants to know why *Christians* think Jews reject Jesus. One needs to understand this from the Jews familiar with the Hebrew language, Jewish tradition, and of course, the Hebrew Bible. But the real question is, do Jews have good reasons for this rejection and would that mean that Christians should reject Jesus as the savior as well? For that answer, one does need to consider the Christian responses and evaluate both arguments to come to a reasonable conclusion, without Judaism or Christianity getting in the way. This is precisely what I did. And you, my faithful reader, will benefit from my exhaustive research.

A messiah in the Jewish tradition simply refers to a leader anointed by God. In the Old Testament (Hebrew Bible), all Kings and even high priests were considers messiahs. A messiah was not God or the Son of God. In short, the future Messiah (capital "M"), as prophesied in the Old Testament, is to be a King of Israel, who will put an end to war by defeating all enemies and bring on an age when everyone knows God. This

Messiah, the Jews believe, is to be a powerful warrior who kicks Gentile buttocks. Never did they expect a man like Jesus who would be seen as a criminal and put to death in the most degrading way. By the looks of it, according to Jews, Jesus was not the Messiah. But Christians disagree.

From the Christian perspective, there are many prophecies in the Old Testament that can be seen as direct evidence that Jesus is the Messiah. He will fulfill those prophecies that he has not fulfilled when he comes back, thus the idea of the "second coming of Christ". Jesus was said to have claimed not just to be the Messiah, but God himself. Christians believe his miracles and being raised from the dead justify this claim. From a less evidential perspective, Jesus is also said to affect the lives of many people today in a very real way. So to Christians, Jesus *is* the Messiah.

While I have looked at just about all arguments (I am sure there are some I missed), made by Jews, against the idea that Jesus is the Messiah, many of them can easily be answered. But there are just a few where the Christian response seemed inadequate or weak. These are the responses we'll examine more closely:

Jesus did not fulfill the messianic prophecies. Jews claim that Jesus did not fulfill the major prophecies such as building the third temple (Ezekiel 37:26-28), gather all Jews back to the land of Israel (Isaiah 43:5-6), usher in an era of world peace, and end all hatred, oppression, suffering and disease (Isaiah 2:4), and spread universal knowledge of the God of Israel, which will unite humanity as one (Zechariah 14:9). But he did ride into town on an ass (Zechariah 9:9). Some Christians believe that Jesus already did fulfill *hundreds* of prophecies, but Jews and other skeptics argue that these "prophecies" are problematic for many reasons as discussed in the chapter on Biblical prophecies.

The second coming is the answer to these major unfulfilled prophecies, however, the Hebrew Bible (OT) makes no reference to the idea of the second coming. The entire idea of this second coming of Jesus was written in the New Testament gospels many years after Jesus' death. Therefore, the idea of the second coming in the New Testament is just self-validation.

The Messiah MUST be a descendant from King David on his father's side (Genesis 49:10 and Isaiah 11:1). If Jesus was from a virgin birth then Joseph is not his father — God is (in a strange, literal "I am my father" sort of way). We know God cannot be a descendant of Kind David. But even if Joseph were the biological father of Jesus, the author of the Gospel of Matthew declares that Jesus was separated from King David by only twenty-eight generations, but in the Gospel of Luke, the list shows a forty-three generation separation. This serious contradiction apparently has been a major issue since early Christianity. There are several possible reasons for this problem proposed over the centuries, all of which are a significant stretch except for one... that neither accounts are accurate. As for *Jesus* being a descendant of King David, one can argue for legitimacy through adoption, but once again, it just doesn't fit. Perhaps the most troubling information I have come across in researching this was a series of letters directed to Pope John Paul II, written by Lawrence Keleman, Professor of Education at Neve Yerushalayim College of Jewish Studies for Women in Jerusalem, raising these issues and looking for a clear explanation. While the Pope did not respond himself, through the Vatican's direction, Keleman was led to Raymond E. Brown, a well-known Catholic theologian who wrote on this very topic. Brown's answers were clear and frank: it was most likely that the *Davidic* genealogy was a fabrication to fulfill that important prophecy. You can find more on this along with scanned copies of the letters from the sources at http://www.simpletoremember.com/vitals/Christian_Credibility.htm .

Only a false prophet would take away the things God told Moses and the prophets. I understand the "new covenant" concept and how Jesus did away with the old and brought in the new. I am down with progress, really! But the Old Testament is quite clear on the unchanging commandments given by God. For example, Deuteronomy 12:32 reads, "Everything I command you that you shall be careful to do it. You shall neither add to it, nor subtract from it." Hundreds of years later, the New Testament is written in a way that subtracts just about all of the 613 Jewish laws commanded by God.

The Jewish scholars, who know their Tanakh (Jewish Bible / Old Testament) extremely well, raise some valid points that should not be dismissed so easily based on Christian interpretation of the Jewish Bible. If Jesus is not the Messiah written about in the Old Testament, it doesn't mean he still wasn't God; it just means Christians have quite a bit of reinterpreting to do. If Jesus is God, then the Jews have some serious work ahead of them. If the prophet Muhammad is right, who says that Jesus was not divine and that anyone who believes he was, is going to Hell (Qur'an Chapter 5 verses 71-75), 85% of America is in big trouble.

Chapter 55: Is the Jesus Story Unique?

In studying world religions, both past and present, I was quite shocked to hear about the many virgin-born, crucified, resurrected, miracle-working, savior-gods who supposedly died for the sins of humanity. As a born and raised Catholic, I knew of only one such man-god that was said to have matched that description. As I researched this area further, I discovered that many books have been written exclusively on this topic. Once I cracked open one of these books, I realized that this "truth" was more complex than I had originally thought. Without question, stories of man-gods with details extremely similar to Jesus', are abundant on the Internet. If even some of these stories were true, it would be convincing evidence that the Jesus story is nothing more than a medley of countless earlier myths, with little or no historical accuracy. So is there truth to these claims?

The first thing we need to do is ask: Where do these stories originate? Virtually all scholars agree that the New Testament documents were written around 60-100 CE. In these documents we are told the "Jesus story" for the first time in the form of Gospels with scattered details appearing in the Letters of Paul. What about the other stories of the other man-gods? Given the literally dozens of similar stories of gods and man-gods circulating today such as *Osiris-Dionysus, Prometheus, Krishna, Buddha, Attis, Mithra*, and others, finding legitimate documents that date to before the time of Jesus is quite a challenge. These stories of Jesus-like figures could easily be fabricated by anti-Christian writers looking to discredit the faith, unless documents pre-dating the New Testament support these claims. It has been suggested that the *Papyrus of Ani*, dated over 1,400 years before

Jesus, mentions some of these similarities with Osiris, and some early poetry and other writings discuss these other gods/man-gods. Scholars who spend their professional careers studying these documents cannot seem to agree as to their age and authenticity, but they don't have to — the truth can be found elsewhere.

Rather than base my research on modern books written to show the similarities between Jesus and other god-like figures before him, I decided to see what some early Christians had to say in defense of this "accusation" since, like virtually all questions about religion, this one is far from new. Early Christian apologist, Justin Martyr (100-165 CE), used these similarities in his *First Apology* (Chapter 22 — dated about 150-155 CE) to help win pagan converts who already accepted the idea of virgin births, crucifixion of man-gods, and miracles. Another Christian Father, Tertullian (160-220 CE) wrote in Chapter 21 of his *Apology* about the similarities with pagan god *Romulus*. It is clear that in these early writings both Christian Fathers accepted, and sometimes even promoted, the similarities to Jesus with other gods and man-gods. So how do they and other early Christian apologists explain these extraordinary similarities? ***Diabolical Mimicry*** (also known as *demonic imitation*). This is the idea that Satan (the devil) started all these rumors about other gods long ago in anticipation of Christ — just so people would have a reason to question the authenticity of the Jesus story (as explained by Justin in Chapter 54 of his apology). I kid you not. This is the best they could come up with.

Is the Jesus story unique? Almost certainly not. I come to this conclusion not by reading anti-Christian books or websites, but by reading the writings of early Christian apologists themselves who were doing their best to defend their faith against the same claims over 1,800 years ago. But just because virgin births, resurrections, savior figures, man-gods, and miracles were more common back then, it does not mean Jesus isn't the real deal; it's just evidence that suggests it's not very likely.

Chapter 56: The Story of Jesus: What Really Happened and Why — According to Me

It's easy for me or anyone to claim that the Christian documents found in the Bible cannot be accepted as a legitimate source of historical fact. The four canonical Gospels were written an estimated 35 to 60 years after the death of Jesus by anonymous authors who never claimed to be eyewitnesses of the events. Plus, these Gospels read more like Greek mythology than historical documents. But this does not mean that the Gospels do not contain historical facts.

Historical facts, in contrast to scientific facts, are less certain due to the subjective nature of researching past events. At one extreme, I can insist that the Gospels are historically accurate, and literal, to every detail, but this assertion works against logic, requires miracles, and is *highly* improbable. At the other extreme, I can deny that Jesus ever existed, but this would lead to numerous inconsistencies with how Christianity developed as well as what the vast majority of serious historical Jesus scholars do accept as historical facts. The truth of the story of Jesus, I suggest, is somewhere in the middle.

Before I get into my reconstruction of the events of 2,000 years ago, be aware that I am not breaking any new ground here. In the last few decades, the availability of dozens of early Christian documents discovered at *Nag Hammadi* (in 1945) gave scholars a new perspective as to how early Christians understood Jesus. Many secular universities began offering courses on religion, which focused on critical study of the texts versus the theological conclusions drawn from theses texts. In recent years, more and more practitioners, including church leaders, began asking important questions, which ultimately led to answers requiring a more liberal theological interpretation of the sacred texts. Interfaith institutions such as the *Westar Institute* were founded to promote the advancement of religious literacy by primarily studying the historical Jesus. Even though many of these scholars consider themselves Christian, they have come to the same conclusion as I have: *the miraculous events associated with Jesus' life were most likely affirmations of faith, rather than historical facts.*

The story begins when Jesus was conceived as a result of his biologically human father having sexual intercourse with his biologically human mother. About 9 months later, he was born. Jesus probably had a normal Jewish childhood, which consisted of education, learning a trade, and getting into trouble. As a Jewish man, Jesus chose to start a ministry preaching a somewhat radical version of the Jewish faith. His rebel-rousing tendencies became a real problem for the authorities and ultimately led to Jesus' execution. Thus ends the story of Jesus. But the *legend* of Jesus had just begun.

About 20 years go by before the first Christian writing, Paul's letter to the Thessalonians, mentions Jesus. While earlier writings most likely did exist, we do not have them. What we do have is four canonical Gospels and many later non-canonical Gospels (some Gnostic) that tell some fantastic, and wildly different stories about Jesus. Given the fact that few people back then could read and write, we know the stories about Jesus were orally passed on for many years in many languages before they were eventually written in Greek. To win converts, Jesus needed to compete with the many pagan gods of the time as well as all the Jewish prophets before him. Throw in some common mythological elements of the day like a virgin birth, miracle stories, and resurrection, and you got yourself the foundation of a new religion worthy of attention. Make Jesus God himself, and now you just one-upped Judaism.

But this simple explanation just won't do. According to religious philosopher and evangelical Christian, Dr. William Lane Craig, there are four "historical facts" which must be explained by any adequate historical hypothesis:

- Jesus' burial
- the discovery of his empty tomb
- his post-mortem appearances
- the origin of the disciples' belief in his resurrection

I'm not sure why he gets to set the rules for determining an "adequate historical hypothesis", but I will do as he commands since he achieved more accolades and degrees in his lifetime than I achieved smiley stickers in mine. But if I may, I am going to reword his "historical facts" to make them actual historical facts:

- Jesus' burial stories as written about in the Gospels and Acts

- the stories of the discovery of his empty tomb as found in the Gospels

- the stories of his post-mortem appearances as found in the New Testament

- the origin of the disciples' belief that Jesus was with God and coming back

Explanation of Fact #1: It is not hard to imagine that Jesus made some wealthy friends in all of his travels. This would explain why his body might have been handed over for a proper burial instead of thrown in a ditch with the other crucified criminals of the day. Jesus was buried; no need for God's help with that one.

Explanation of Fact #2: Although it may be seen as inadequate to say that the empty tomb stories were a later creation to affirm the faith, I am sticking with that very likely explanation. This would explain why Paul, in none of his letters, mentions an empty tomb. Paul believed in a spiritual resurrection, not a physical one.

Explanation of Fact #3: It is very important to note that **Paul is the only New Testament writer who claims to have seen the risen Jesus himself**. Paul's own first-hand testimony of this (*1 Corinthians 15:3-8*) is very lackluster with no details of how Jesus appeared to him. When Paul's vision is described in Acts Chapter 9 by someone who most scholars believe to be a follower of Paul, it's very magical, but nothing like seeing a physical person. The detailed stories of the resurrected Jesus whippin' up breakfast for the old gang develop 35 to 60 years after Jesus' death. To this day, visions of loved ones who have passed away are very common and have very good naturalistic explanations. Even if you believe that ghost sightings are of a supernatural nature, you probably would agree that they are not gods.

Explanation of Fact #4: Imagine you gave up everything, sold all your possessions, hated your family (Luke 14:26), and devoted three years of your life to this man who you thought was the promised Messiah sent from God. This is the man, according to the Jewish scriptures, who would bring justice to the Jews. Then, he is killed. You can admit you might have been wrong about this Jesus guy, or you can reason that he MUST be coming back to finish the job. Nobody likes to admit they were wrong, especially when it's possible that they can still be right.

From this point on, it took several hundred years to work out an "orthodox" story of Jesus that serves as the foundation of Christianity to this day. The early church fathers couldn't even do it without introducing paradoxes and logical impossibilities that still trouble many Christian philosophers and theologians today. Yet most practicing Christians have no trouble accepting Jesus as 100% man and 100% God, or the doctrine of the Trinity (three persons in one), neither of which are mentioned anywhere in the Bible.

Christianity never had to deal with the kind of modern textual criticism practiced today. Super-fast computers, global information sharing, and the growing number of secular universities offering programs in religious study all pose an increasing challenge to what was once virtually undisputed Biblical fact. As it becomes increasingly difficult for moderate Christians to ignore the differences between the historical Jesus and the theological Jesus, we will witness Christianity enter in its next phase of evolution.

PART IX: MAKING SENSE OF IT ALL

Chapter 57: Does God Exist?

Without question God exists. To some, God exists only as a fairy-tale. To others, God is a spiritual being who contains many human characteristics along with many divine characteristics, which makes him an infinite being; i.e., a being without limits, who is the creator of everything, engages in personal relationships with people, and is something we must worship or taste his wrath. Put in these terms, everyone believes in God; it's just a matter of where one puts God on this epistemological spectrum.

If it hasn't been blatantly clear by now, I am extremely confident that the God of the Bible does not exist. I have used evidence, logic, reason, and critical thinking to demonstrate how the God of the Bible is *extremely* improbable. But this Biblical idea of God is just one of many views of God held by theists. In addition to the Biblical God, there is the *creator* God, the *experiential* God, and the *spiritual* God. Let's examine the possible existence of all three.

First, let's look at the sheer possibility of a non-material being's existence that we can apply to all three Gods. We know God is not made from matter, and we know that non-material existence is possible outside of the human mind. Energy, plus forces such as gravity, magnetic forces, and nuclear forces are all non-material things that exist independent of us. That is, they exist with or without us needing to exist. We know through scientific testing and observation that energy and forces do interact with the material world. It is very likely that forms of energy and/or forces exist that we have not scientifically discovered. But to classify such a form or energy or force as a *being,* that is, a life force with a mind and consciousness crosses the line of reasonable probability to a leap of faith.

Does a creator God exist? Along with theists, *deists* believe one does. Deists are people who believe that a supreme being, often referred to as God, created the universe and that's it. This God is also referred to as the *First Cause* or *Prime Mover*. It's possible that such a force exists, outside the boundaries of space and time, which set our universe in motion. But this is pure speculation. If this scenario is possible, then it's also possible that the universe is a result of many forces. Or that the forces which sparked the creation of the universe are ones we know of that exist in our universe today. The idea I described in the chapter, "The Fine Tuning Argument" about the creation of everything not requiring any rules to follow or parameters to finely tune, leads to the conclusion that no intelligent being or even just a "being" was required to set the universe in motion. Therefore, a creator-type God, is not needed, and most likely doesn't exist.

Does an *experiential* God exist? In this book, we looked at spirituality and how people interpret religious experiences. We have seen that people from all over the world "experience God" in many different ways — so different, in fact, that many of these experiences are explained without any kind of god. People's cultural backgrounds play a crucial role in how they interpret their religious experiences. In the United States, where over 85% of the population is Christian, religious experiences frequently lead those who had the experience to the immediate conclusion that Jesus is the Son of God and the Christian Bible is all true. This is not because of divine revelation, but because of human association. People most likely don't experience "God"; they experience feelings and emotions that they associate with God. Therefore, an experiential God most likely does not exist.

Does a *spiritual* God exist? Many theists insist that one can never get to know God through "worldly things" such as logic, reason, or even knowledge. Science, philosophy, biology, and anything else of this world will never lead you to an understanding of God. Even our minds are incapable of comprehending God. Philosophically speaking, this makes a lot of sense. But those who hold this belief do not just stop there. They claim to "know" God spiritually, which takes us to the experiential God and the associated problems with that God's existence. Unless we posit a spiritual realm of existence where the spirit can "know" things (somehow it needs a brain-like thing of its own), we can only "know" God using our human brain, which is part of this material world and not compatible with God — like trying to run that latest Windows® operating system on a

1982 Commodore 64. Any effort we make to imagine this God, explain this God, or especially to write books about this God, is nothing more than an inadequate attempt to explain the unexplainable. Furthermore, those who believe in this spiritual God claim that he interacts with the material world, yet continue to insist that we cannot use constructs of the material world such as science or logic to validate the existence of this spiritual God. If the spiritual God does exist in some spiritual realm that is so far beyond our understanding, he doesn't interact with this world, and we are only deceived by our minds in believing we are communicating with this spiritual God. However, it's very likely that a spiritual God does not exist.

But there is a God that DOES exist, and that is the *conceptual* God. A concept is an abstract idea that exists *dependent on a mind* — in this case, the human mind. Concepts are very real, and can have very real effects on our inner and outer world. Perhaps the most common and simple Christian definition of God is, "God is love". Love, like God, is a concept that has no existence apart from the being experiencing the love. When people say, "Love is in the air," that's not a statement of fact. As a concept, God is subjective, which allows "him" to be all things to all people. God is a reflection of our own subjective sense of perfection. To the ancient Hebrews, God was an undefeatable, vengeful, warrior God who brought justice to "his people". To many of today's Christians, God is pure love and forgiveness (except when it comes to those who don't believe in him, of course).

I do believe God exists; yet I consider myself a nontheist because I do not accept the many properties and actions that are generally accepted as part of the theistic God. God is not a person, not a being, but a concept that we have created and continue to create. Simply put, God is "The Concept".

Chapter 58: Conclusion

Religion, like it or not, is a major part of our history, culture, and daily lives. Religion is not going anywhere — not until the major questions about life are answered to everyone's complete satisfaction. Atheists find satisfaction in naturalistic explanations and see the unknown as an opportunity for further exploration. Theists posit God as an intelligent being responsible for the universe and everything in it, while finding satisfaction in the continual process of getting to know this God. No matter what label we may give ourselves, we are all part of the human race seeking a better understanding of our world and our place in it.

Unfortunately, different beliefs can lead to conflict. The more powerful and important the belief, the more serious the conflict, especially when the belief is knowledge of the one and only "Truth" that cannot be proven, but only accepted on faith. History has some fascinating, yet horrible, stories to tell as a result of this kind of belief. Today, although this problem is far from resolved, better communication, public debate, and a more welcoming dialogue have led to a greater tolerance and understanding of religious differences. This trend can only continue when people open their minds to other ideas, people, and new information.

In this book, I proposed understanding God as a concept existing in our minds, rather than as a supreme being with direct physical control over our world. I see this understanding of God as one that frees us from the archaic and superstitious bonds of religion, while empowering us from within, without the need for supernatural help. But to many people, this radical move in the understanding of God may be seen just as moving to a life without God. To that, I leave you with these final words.

A life without God is not a life without meaning; it is a life where you are free to define your own meaning.

A life without God is not a life without faith; it is a life where you have faith in humanity.

A life without God is not a life without moral values; it is a life with all the moral values you choose to hold.

A life without God is not a life without hope; it is a life where hope is dependent upon the natural world and the beings in it.

A life without God is not a life without spirituality; it is a life where spirituality is taking control of your emotions and feelings.

A life without God is not a life without Jesus; it is life of accepting Jesus as the person he most likely was, rather than the person you want him to be.

A life without God is not a life without Christianity; it is a life that admires and celebrates the aspects Christianity independent of a supernatural being.

A life without God is not a life without God. God the being may not exist, but God "The Concept" always will.

~~~ * ~~~

Letter To God

Dear God,

I do not believe that you exist like the Bible says you do, but just in case I am incorrect, I want you to know why I came to the conclusion I did, so that if Hell exists, you don't make me go there.

I have read your book, the Bible, cover to cover, with an open heart and an open mind. I have read many books about you from both atheist and Christian authors. I did what Christians suggest and asked you, in prayer, to reveal yourself to me. Well, you didn't. In addition, the mind that you have given me, along with my understanding of logic, reason, and common sense, has led me to the conclusion that you do not exist outside of our minds.

I will continue to live my life according to the moral and ethical standards that are within me, whether there by evolution, society, or placed there by you. If this is not good enough for you, I accept my final destination next to other non-believers of you, like Gandhi, Buddha, and the billions of other kind, loving, and often spiritual people who just happened to pick the wrong religion.

Thank you in advance for your understanding, and thank you for everything (literally).

Your Creation,

Bo Bennett

Bibliography

Books

The Holy Bible. New International Version, Michigan: Zondervan, 2009.

Bernard Brandon Scott, comps. and eds. The Resurrection of Jesus. Santa Rosa, CA: Polebridge Press, 2008.

Charles W. Hedrick, comps. and eds. When Faith Meets Reason. Santa Rosa, CA: Polebridge Press, 2008.

Dawkins, Richard. The God Delusion. New York, NY: Mariner Books, 2008.

D'Souza, Dinesh. What's So Great About Christianity. New York, NY: Tyndale House Publishers, Inc., 2008.

Ehrman, Bart D. Misquoting Jesus. New York, NY: HarperOne, 2007.

Freke, Timothy, and Peter Gandy. The Jesus Mysteries. New York, NY: Three Rivers Press, 2001.

Harris, Sam. Letter to a Christian Nation. New York, NY: Vintage, 2008.

Hawking, Stephen. A Briefer History of Time. New York, NY: Bantam, 2008.

Lewis, C.S. Mere Christianity. New York, NY: HarperOne, 2001.

Newburg, Andrew. Why We Believe What We Believe: Uncovering Our Biological Need for Meaning, Spirituality, and Truth. New York, NY: Free Press, 2006.

Robert J. Miller, comps. and eds. The Complete Gospels. Santa Rosa, CA: Polebridge Press, 1994.

Shermer, Michael. How We Believe: The Search for God In an Age of Science. New York, NY: W.H. Freeman & Company, 1999.

Strobel, Lee. The Case for Christ: A Journalist's Personal Investigation of the Evidence for Jesus. Michigan: Zondervan, 1998.

Tippett, Krista. Einstein's God. New York, NY: Penguin Books, 2010.

Walsch, Neale Donald. Conversations With God. New York, NY: Putnam Adult, 1996.

Wright, Robert. The Evolution of God. New York, NY: Back Bay Books, 2010.

Courses

The following courses were produced by the Teaching Company. They can be found online at http://www.teach12.com

After the New Testament: The Writings of the Apostolic Fathers, Prof. Bart D. Ehrman, 12 hours

American Religious History, Prof. Patrick N. Allitt, 12 hours

Argumentation: The Study of Effective Reasoning, 2nd Edition, Prof. David Zarefsky, 12 hours

Big History: The Big Bang, Life on Earth, and the Rise of Humanity, Prof. David Christian, 24 hours

The Catholic Church: A History, Prof. William R. Cook, 18 hours

Darwinian Revolution, Prof. Frederick Gregory, 12 hours

Dead Sea Scrolls, Prof. Gary A. Rendsburg, 12 hours

From Jesus to Constantine: A History of Early Christianity, Prof. Bart D. Ehrman, 12 hours

Great Philosophical Debates: Free Will and Determinism, Prof. Shaun Nichols, 12 hours

Great World Religions: Christianity, Prof. Luke Timothy Johnson, 6 hours

History of the Bible: The Making of the New Testament Canon, Prof. Bart D. Ehrman, 6 hours

Lost Christianities: Christian Scriptures and the Battles over Authentication, Prof. Bart D. Ehrman, 12 hours

New Testament, Prof. Bart D. Ehrman, 12 hours

Old Testament, Prof. Amy-Jill Levine, 12 hours

Particle Physics for Non-Physicists: A Tour of the Microcosmos, Prof. Steven Pollock, 12 hours

Philosophy and Religion in the West, Prof. Phillip Cary, 12 hours

Philosophy of Mind: Brains, Consciousness, and Thinking Machines, Prof. Patrick Grim, 12 hours

Skeptics and Believers: Religious Debate in the Western Intellectual Tradition, Prof. Tyler Roberts, 18 hours

Story of the Bible, Prof. Luke Timothy Johnson, 12 hours

Theory of Evolution: A History of Controversy, Prof. Edward J. Larson, 6 hours

The following courses were found on iTunes Univerisity.

Apologetics, Emmaus Online, Prof. Mark Stevenson, 20 hours

Introduction to New Testament History and Literature, Yale University, Prof. Dale B. Martin, 19 hours

Historical Jesus, Stanford University, Prof. Thomas Sheehan, 18 hours

Debates

Over a thousand hours of debates can be found at http:// www.DebateGod.org. This site is owned and operated by yours truly.

About The Author

Robert (Bo) Bennett is a business man, author, programmer, philosopher, martial artist, motivational speaker, amateur comedian, and most of all a husband and a father devoted to improving the lives of others. He is a graduate of Bryant College with a Bachelors degree in Marketing.

By age 10, Bo started listening to and reading personal development tapes and books. Twenty years and hundreds of books later he is considered by many to be one of the leading experts on success. Before beginning his lifelong quest to shape the lives of others, he had to prove to himself that his theories, beliefs and convictions worked.

At age 10, Bo started in business by creating and selling wooden key racks in his father's workshop. Since then, he has started several companies and sold them anywhere from $1 to $20,000,000.00. Today, Bo remains active President of Archieboy Holdings, LLC.

At age 13, Bo started studying the martial arts. By Age 18, he earned his first degree black belt in Shaolin Kempo Karate. Since his first black belt, he has also earned a second degree black belt in Tae-Kwon Do and continues to study several different styles, as well as teach. When starting the martial arts, Bo also began a lifelong commitment to fitness and health, realizing the importance of the mind-body connection.

After selling his first company of significant value, Bo began writing Year To Success, the most comprehensive book ever written on success, based on his experiences, thoughts, and timeless success principles. Year to Success is a book Donald Trump calls, "an inspiration to every person who reads it."

Bo is also a major supporter of and contributor to Toastmasters International (toastmasters.org), an organization established in 1924 to promote communication and leadership through public speaking.

Bo and his wife, Kim, reside in Massachusetts with their two young children and their faithful dog.

Book Description

Maybe you were born to Christian parents and raised as a Christian. Or maybe you are just a part of a Christian nation. You might have attended church regularly, or maybe just on special occasions. If asked, you say that you believe in God, but you really never thought about what that means exactly. You are a well-educated person who accepts the idea of Biblical miracles, but only the more "reasonable" ones. You have read some of the Bible, mostly just parts of the New Testament, but never committed to reading the Bible cover to cover. You are a good person who admires the many "Christian values" as demonstrated by Jesus Christ. But something does not feel right.

- Science tells us that the universe is **13.7 billion years old**, but the Bible tells us it's **6,000 years old**.

- Science tells us life is the result of **emergent properties in combined molecules**, and we have evolved from a very primitive life form, but the Bible says that **God made us, as is, from dust, and blew life in our noses**.

- You see a world where **little bunnies burn to death in forest fires**, and wonder why an all-good and loving God would allow such a thing to happen.

- You pray to God and you realize that sometimes your prayers are answered, and sometimes they aren't — **just as if you didn't pray at all.**

- You hear about other religions and wonder why your religion is right and **every other religion on the planet is wrong**.

- You have a real problem with the idea of all your non-Jesus-believing friends and family **spending eternity in Hell**.

In fact, the more you look around, the more you see a world absent of this perfect image of a perfect God. As much as you want to avoid critical thinking and "just let go and have faith", you find that you cannot believe in something contrary to your logic and reason — no matter how much you want to. This might lead to feelings of guilt, insincerity, and/or hypocrisy. Yet you just can't imagine living life without God, *and you don't have to.*

When you start asking serious questions about God and religion, you begin to see through the stories of people living inside the stomachs of big fish, 900-year-old men, and bodies coming back to life after three days, and understand how man created God, and not the other way around. By daring to question "sacred" religion, challenging your childhood beliefs, and risking eternal damnation (okay, so there might be a minor side effect to reading this book), you will discover an appreciation for religion on a new level, as well as a renewed appreciation for the human race.

Through a unique blend of science, philosophy, theology, and a touch of humor, you will see how you can trust your logic and reason, be true to yourself, and embrace God -- not as a being, but as a concept -- *The Concept.*

CPSIA information can be obtained
at www.ICGtesting.com
Printed in the USA
BVHW04s0138040518
515048BV00037B/879/P